Health Care

Opposing Viewpoints®

OTHER BOOKS OF RELATED INTEREST

OPPOSING VIEWPOINTS SERIES

AIDS
Biomedical Ethics
Death & Dying
Epidemics
Euthanasia
Genetic Engineering
Health and Fitness
Inequality: Opposing Viewpoints in Social Problems
Mental Illness

CURRENT CONTROVERSIES SERIES

Assisted Suicide
The Disabled
Medical Ethics
Reproductive Technologies

AT ISSUE SERIES

Cloning
The Ethics of Euthanasia
Physician-Assisted Suicide

Health Care

Opposing Viewpoints®

James D. Torr, Book Editor

David L. Bender, Publisher

Bruno Leone, Executive Editor

Bonnie Szumski, Editorial Director

David M. Haugen, Managing Editor

OPPOSING
VIEWPOINTS®
SERIES

Greenhaven Press, Inc., San Diego, California

Cover photo: Corbis Corp.

Library of Congress Cataloging-in-Publication Data

Health care : opposing viewpoints / James D. Torr, book editor.
     p.   cm. — (Opposing viewpoints series)
    Includes bibliographical references and index.
    ISBN 0-7377-0128-5 (pbk. : alk. paper). —
ISBN 0-7377-0129-3 (lib. : alk. paper)
    1. Primary health care. I. Torr, James D., 1974–   . II. Series:
Opposing viewpoints series (Unnumbered)
RA427.9.H39 2000
362.1—dc21   98-55105
                                                    CIP

Greenhaven Press, Inc., P.O. Box 289009
San Diego, CA 92198-9009

"CONGRESS SHALL MAKE NO LAW...ABRIDGING THE FREEDOM OF SPEECH, OR OF THE PRESS."

First Amendment to the U.S. Constitution

The basic foundation of our democracy is the First Amendment guarantee of freedom of expression. The Opposing Viewpoints Series is dedicated to the concept of this basic freedom and the idea that it is more important to practice it than to enshrine it.

CONTENTS

Chapter 3: What Government Initiatives Could Improve the Health Care System?

Chapter 4: How Should the United States Reform Its Health Care System?

WHY CONSIDER OPPOSING VIEWPOINTS?

"The only way in which a human being can make some approach to knowing the whole of a subject is by hearing what can be said about it by persons of every variety of opinion and studying all modes in which it can be looked at by every character of mind. No wise man ever acquired his wisdom in any mode but this."

John Stuart Mill

In our media-intensive culture it is not difficult to find differing opinions. Thousands of newspapers and magazines and dozens of radio and television talk shows resound with differing points of view. The difficulty lies in deciding which opinion to agree with and which "experts" seem the most credible. The more inundated we become with differing opinions and claims, the more essential it is to hone critical reading and thinking skills to evaluate these ideas. Opposing Viewpoints books address this problem directly by presenting stimulating debates that can be used to enhance and teach these skills. The varied opinions contained in each book examine many different aspects of a single issue. While examining these conveniently edited opposing views, readers can develop critical thinking skills such as the ability to compare and contrast authors' credibility, facts, argumentation styles, use of persuasive techniques, and other stylistic tools. In short, the Opposing Viewpoints Series is an ideal way to attain the higher-level thinking and reading skills so essential in a culture of diverse and contradictory opinions.

In addition to providing a tool for critical thinking, Opposing Viewpoints books challenge readers to question their own strongly held opinions and assumptions. Most people form their opinions on the basis of upbringing, peer pressure, and personal, cultural, or professional bias. By reading carefully balanced opposing views, readers must directly confront new ideas as well as the opinions of those with whom they disagree. This is not to simplistically argue that everyone who reads opposing views will—or should—change his or her opinion. Instead, the series enhances readers' understanding of their own views by encouraging confrontation with opposing ideas. Careful examination of others' views can lead to the readers' understanding of the logical inconsistencies in their own opinions, perspective on why they hold an opinion, and the consideration of the possibility that their opinion requires further evaluation.

EVALUATING OTHER OPINIONS

To ensure that this type of examination occurs, Opposing Viewpoints books present all types of opinions. Prominent spokespeople on different sides of each issue as well as well-known professionals from many disciplines challenge the reader. An additional goal of the series is to provide a forum for other, less known, or even unpopular viewpoints. The opinion of an ordinary person who has had to make the decision to cut off life support from a terminally ill relative, for example, may be just as valuable and provide just as much insight as a medical ethicist's professional opinion. The editors have two additional purposes in including these less known views. One, the editors encourage readers to respect others' opinions—even when not enhanced by professional credibility. It is only by reading or listening to and objectively evaluating others' ideas that one can determine whether they are worthy of consideration. Two, the inclusion of such viewpoints encourages the important critical thinking skill of objectively evaluating an author's credentials and bias. This evaluation will illuminate an author's reasons for taking a particular stance on an issue and will aid in readers' evaluation of the author's ideas.

As series editors of the Opposing Viewpoints Series, it is our hope that these books will give readers a deeper understanding of the issues debated and an appreciation of the complexity of even seemingly simple issues when good and honest people disagree. This awareness is particularly important in a democratic society such as ours in which people enter into public debate to determine the common good. Those with whom one disagrees should not be regarded as enemies but rather as people whose views deserve careful examination and may shed light on one's own.

Thomas Jefferson once said that "difference of opinion leads to inquiry, and inquiry to truth." Jefferson, a broadly educated man, argued that "if a nation expects to be ignorant and free . . . it expects what never was and never will be." As individuals and as a nation, it is imperative that we consider the opinions of others and examine them with skill and discernment. The Opposing Viewpoints Series is intended to help readers achieve this goal.

David L. Bender & Bruno Leone,
Series Editors

Greenhaven Press anthologies primarily consist of previously published material taken from a variety of sources, including periodicals, books, scholarly journals, newspapers, government documents, and position papers from private and public organizations. These original sources are often edited for length and to ensure their accessibility for a young adult audience. The anthology editors also change the original titles of these works in order to clearly present the main thesis of each viewpoint and to explicitly indicate the opinion presented in the viewpoint. These alterations are made in consideration of both the reading and comprehension levels of a young adult audience. Every effort is made to ensure that Greenhaven Press accurately reflects the original intent of the authors included in this anthology.

INTRODUCTION

"America's health care system is neither healthy, caring, nor a system."

—Walter Cronkite, journalist

"It is a lot easier to find gaps in the health care system than to find ways to fill them."

—Willis D. Gradison, U.S. congressman

The United States has the most advanced health care system in the world. Each year doctors and scientists make incredible innovations in treating disease and injury, and each year thousands of people travel to the United States to take advantage of its prestigious doctors, hospitals, and treatment centers. Most criticism of the health care system, therefore, is concerned not with its relatively high quality, but with its increasingly high cost.

Americans spend roughly a trillion dollars on health care each year—over 13 percent of the gross domestic product. Health care spending more than doubled between 1975 and 1985, and doubled again between 1985 and 1995. If it continues to climb at this rate, experts fear that it could bankrupt the nation. Although health care inflation is often presented as a national problem, higher medical bills result in higher health insurance premiums, which are ultimately paid for by individuals.

Various explanations have been offered for the vexing problem of health care inflation. Some experts blame expensive medical technologies, while others emphasize that, partly because life expectancy has increased, Americans today are, on average, older than previous generations, and thus more likely to need health services. Critics have charged that there are too many doctors; that doctors are overpaid; that drug companies overprice their pharmaceuticals; and that government safety regulations drive up the price of new medicines. Some believe that hundreds of private insurance plans and government programs have made the health care system so complex that a large portion of health care costs is wasted on administrative paperwork. Finally, many observers maintain that, because health is so important to most people, there is no limit to the amount they are willing to pay to live longer or feel healthier.

Whatever its causes, health care inflation has a profound effect on the health care system: The United States offers the best medical care in the world, but a growing number of Americans are unable to afford it. As insurance premiums rose in the 1980s, health coverage became too expensive for many individuals, and many employers, who usually pay a large part of their employees' health insurance, stopped offering coverage altogether. Twenty-four million Americans lacked any form of health insurance in 1980; this figure reached 36 million in 1990 and has continued to grow by about one million per year since then.

In the early 1990s, many believed that these problems had reached crisis proportions. When President Bill Clinton took office in January 1993, he made health care reform a top priority. Clinton resolved that his health care reform plan would institute universal coverage—that is, provide health insurance for all Americans.

Clinton named his wife, Hillary, and policy analyst Ira Magaziner to lead the Task Force on National Health Care Reform. The 1,342-page plan they eventually released was complex and not widely understood at first. It would have provided universal coverage mainly by requiring all employers to provide health insurance to their employees and by subsidizing coverage for the unemployed. To control costs, the plan would have introduced a system of "managed competition," in which private insurers would compete for the business of health alliances—groups of businesses and individual consumers that were to be established in each state.

At the time, support for health care reform seemed widespread. The Clinton plan, however, became the center of enormous controversy for more than a year. Republicans charged that the plan would introduce a huge amount of bureaucracy and inefficiency into the health care system, and Democrats disagreed over many of the plan's specifics. The insurance industry launched an ad campaign in which a fictional couple, "Harry and Louise," warned the public that the plan would not let people choose their own doctor and would lead to "socialized medicine." These commercials articulated fears that many people had about the Clinton plan; eventually public support for health care reform dwindled, and the Clinton plan finally died in congressional committee late in 1994.

Exactly why the Clinton plan attracted so much opposition remains a subject of considerable controversy today. Many feel that the Clinton plan represented, in the words of economist Clifford F. Thies, "a complete government takeover of health care," and that the public was right to reject it. Others believe that Clinton's plan was rejected because it would have harmed the profits of doctors, private insurers, and pharmaceutical companies. Author Nicholas Laham charges that "members of Congress of both parties are heavily dependent upon campaign contributions from the health care industry to win reelection."

For whatever reason, Clinton's plan was rejected—but the problems it was supposed to address have not gone away. Employers, upset with how much money they were paying for health coverage, turned to health maintenance organizations, or HMOs, to control costs. HMOs are a type of managed care organization, and usually offer lower rates than traditional health plans do. Roughly 60 million Americans are now part of some type of managed care plan.

In theory, managed care keeps costs down by providing cost-efficient care and keeping patients healthy with preventive medicine. In 1996, however, media coverage of health care began to be dominated by managed care "horror stories" in which people died because their HMO refused to pay for expensive life-saving treatment. Other charges that HMOs have misdiagnosed patients or skimped on care now have people worrying about the quality of their health care as well as its cost.

Some critics also worry that managed care will not be as successful in controlling costs as was once hoped. Although health care costs did decrease from 1994 to 1995 (for the first time in ten years), since then they have again begun to climb. And as health care costs rise, the number of uninsured increases: The Census Bureau reports that 43.4 million people, or 16 percent of the population, went without health insurance throughout 1997.

Although interest in health care reform among politicians and the media has dwindled since 1994, many observers contend that the problems of the health care system have gotten worse, not better, since then. In this view, rising health care costs, problems with managed care, and large numbers of uninsured people will continue to plague the health care system until comprehensive health care reform is once again on the political agenda. The authors in Health Care: Opposing Viewpoints debate these issues in the following chapters: Is America's Health Care System in Need of Reform? How Has Managed Care Affected the Health Care System? What Government Initiatives Could Improve the Health Care System? How Should the United States Reform Its Health Care System? By examining a wide variety of opinions, it is hoped that the reader will gain a better understanding of why health care reform is such a sensitive issue in American politics.

IS AMERICA'S HEALTH CARE SYSTEM IN NEED OF REFORM?

CHAPTER PREFACE

One of the major problems facing the health care system is that Americans are growing older. There were 31.1 million Americans over age 65 in 1990; this figure is expected to more than double by 2025. Not only will the aging of the baby boom generation—the large number of Americans born shortly after World War II—result in more elderly people, who tend to need more health care, but older persons will also make up a much larger *percentage* of the population. Simply put, there will be more people in need of health care, and fewer who are able to provide and pay for it.

Some observers believe this demographic change will pose an unaffordable burden on the U.S. economy. Currently, more than one third of health expenditures are spent on the 12 percent of the population aged 65 and older. Some studies estimate that as much as 30 percent of Medicare expenditures go to treat people in the last year of life. At this rate, it is argued, health care costs for the elderly will bankrupt the nation.

However, others believe such fears are exaggerated. They contend that several European countries already have the age structure that the United States is projected to have, but still have managed to control health care costs. In its report *Seven Deadly Myths*, the Alliance for Aging Research cites statistics indicating that less is spent on health care for the elderly than is widely believed. Moreover, the report notes that blaming the elderly for health care inflation does little to help the health care system. The alliance quotes health economist Thomas E. Getzen:

> If rising health care costs are due to aging and other external forces, then they are not "my" responsibility, nor can they be blamed on doctors, hospitals, insurance companies, governments, or indeed any of the institutions which should, in fact, be held responsible. By making it seem as if increases are inevitable, attention is diverted from the real and difficult choices that must be made and the institutions which make them.

Most experts agree that the "aging of America" will exacerbate the problems of health care inflation and the uninsured. However, as the authors in the following chapter will demonstrate, aging baby boomers are not the only challenge the health care system faces. The authors in this chapter debate the extent to which these problems are putting the health care system in crisis.

"Too many politicians, corporate financial officers and academic economists tend to forget the most basic truth about medical care in America: We have the finest system for treating illnesses and injuries in the world."

AMERICA HAS THE BEST HEALTH CARE SYSTEM IN THE WORLD

Joseph A. Califano Jr.

America has the finest health care system in the world, argues Joseph A. Califano Jr. in the following viewpoint. He describes how scientists, government, and corporations have all helped to improve the health care system, but also warns that some health care reforms may threaten the progress that has been made. Califano insists that, in their quest to reduce health care costs, doctors, politicians, and insurers must also preserve those aspects of the health care system that have made it so successful. Califano is a former U.S. secretary of health, education, and welfare, and the president of the National Center on Addiction and Substance Abuse at Columbia University.

As you read, consider the following questions:
1. In what year was the Public Health Service established?
2. In the author's view, under what two presidents did biomedical research in America begin to thrive?
3. Why did Congress pass Medicare and Medicaid, according to Califano?

Reprinted from Joseph A. Califano Jr., "Healthy Horizons," The American Legion Magazine, September 1997, by permission of the author.

There is a wise old African proverb from the Bassuto tribe that Robert Ruark appropriated for his book on the Mau Mau uprisings of the 1950s: Do not destroy something of value unless you have something of value to replace it.

THE ENVY OF THE WORLD

That proverb should be a warning signal and guiding principle for those who have set about the delicate task of changing America's health-care system. With all the sound and fury about the state of health care in America, too many politicians, corporate financial officers and academic economists tend to forget the most basic truth about medical care in America: We have the finest system for treating illnesses and injuries in the world. American physicians, hospitals, research centers and medical schools are the envy of the world. Heads of state and foreigners with the unlimited wealth to pay any price for the best care available flock to the United States when they are sick.

The 1990s have been marked by a headlong rush for efficiency in delivering treatment to sick and injured Americans; recognition by the for-profit sector of the big bucks to be made in taking care of what ails us; determination by the federal government to trim back funds spent on Medicare, Medicaid and other health programs for research and training if that is what it takes to balance the budget; aggressive actions by downsizing corporations to reduce costs of providing health-care benefits to employees; and increased pressures on pharmaceutical companies to reduce the price of their products even if that means forcing them to cut back on applied research.

THREATENING THE PROGRESS THAT HAS BEEN MADE

Taken separately, something can be said for variations of each of these trends. Taken together, they threaten the world-class greatness that has characterized America's medical-treatment system for most of this century.

It's time for each of us to look at what made America's health-care system the finest in the world and demand that those who would dramatically restructure it count to 10 before they lose sight of the conditions that made our system great.

What makes America's health-care system great is its ability to attract the finest minds in our society to devote their lives to caring for the ill and to conducting research to attack seemingly intractable medical problems. Also critical to the special quality of care here is the commitment of doctors and nurses to health care as a ministry, not an industry. It wasn't always this way.

At the end of the last century and into the early years of the 20th century, American medicine was crowded with charlatans and hustlers. Doctors were poorly trained. Many medical schools were as wacky in what they taught as a Three Stooges movie. Traveling salesmen hawked potions laced with cocaine that hooked thousands of Midwest housewives who thought they were buying relief for everything from arthritis and menstrual cramps to depression and heart disease.

Then, in 1910, Abraham Flexner exposed the false claims, shoddy curriculum, facilities and faculties of many medical schools. Shocked into action by the public outcry and supported by the good physicians, states passed laws instituting stiff licensing requirements and high standards for doctors and the medical schools that trained them.

About this time, states also enacted statutes severely restricting the practice of medicine to licensed physicians, and Congress established the Food and Drug Administration and gave it the power to test medications to make certain they were safe and effective before they could be marketed to Americans.

As a result of these actions, the quality of medical education and physicians soared. Doctors whose average 19th century income put them in the lower middle class, rose rapidly in economic and social status in their communities. The words, "my son the doctor," became the prayer and dream of a generation of immigrants. And the best and the brightest men and women were attracted to the medical profession.

THE FDA AND THE PUBLIC HEALTH SERVICE

Over time, thanks to the system of clearing pharmaceuticals by the FDA, this nation avoided tragedies that beset other countries. In Britain, for example, thousands of children were born deformed as a result of mothers taking thalidomide. We avoided that situation—and others like it—here because of the tough review requirements to which drugs were subjected before they could be prescribed by physicians or sold over the counter. More than any other people in the world, Americans could be confident that the medicine they were given would work and that those medicines would be safe to take.

In the earliest days of the Republic—1789—we established a Public Health Service. At the turn of the 20th century, Congress began expanding the mission of the Public Health Service to include the study of infectious diseases and control of epidemics. But the role of the national government in public health and biomedical research was marginal up to World War II.

As part of the nation's mobilization for World War II, the federal government made substantial investments in public health, training professionals and medical research. The armed forces needed physicians and nurses, so they drafted all they could get their hands on and trained even more. Medical research was conducted on everything from frostbite to malaria, from venereal disease to surgical and burn procedures. Public health programs were mounted to protect soldiers from sexually transmitted diseases and keep production workers on the home front healthy and strong. Wonder drugs like penicillin, new surgical procedures for wounds and burns and prosthetic devices to replace lost limbs were developed.

PRIVATE ENTERPRISE BENEFITS PUBLIC HEALTH

America's competitive impulse generates medical innovation not only for American consumers but for the entire world. About half the world's output of medical devices occurs in the United States, and private research and development spending by U.S. pharmaceutical and device manufacturers dwarfs that of other nations. And despite the fact that other countries with less market-oriented economies benefit from U.S. medical innovations, Americans still enjoy more access to quality health care than virtually any other nation, according to studies by the journal *Health Affairs* and others. . . .

Private enterprise contributes to our health in an even more basic way than advancing drug research or promoting technological change. Because the U.S. economy provides basic goods and services at relatively low cost, families can afford to spend more to improve their lives. From 1960 to 1992, real spending on food as a share of GDP [gross domestic product] fell by nearly a third, as technological innovations helped farmers increase their productivity and reduce spoilage. Spending on clothes stayed constant during the same period. These trends freed up household income for services such as discretionary medical care and recreation. By generating unprecedented economic production, our economy has given families the financial wherewithal to purchase medical services and otherwise improve their health in a way that our grandparents and great-grandparents would find truly mind-boggling.

John Hood, *Policy Review*, November/December 1996.

At the end of the war, the military research effort was transferred to the National Institutes of Health. In the post-war years, these institutes became the central workhorse for basic biomedical research. Sparked by the bipartisan commitment of Presidents

Lyndon Johnson and Richard Nixon, who declared billion-dollar-a-year wars on cancer and cardiovascular disease, the National Institutes of Health and the National Cancer Institute became the finest basic biomedical research operation in the world. The brightest scientists in the United States and many foreign nations competed either to work there or to receive grants to work at research centers throughout the nation.

In the 1940s and 1950s most large corporations started including health insurance coverage as part of their basic wage and benefits package, and the government built half a million hospital beds. In the 1960s, with President Johnson calling upon Americans to create a Great Society, Congress passed Medicare to provide physician and hospital care for all citizens 65 and older and Medicaid to provide such care to the poor and nursing home care to the elderly who needed it. Congress enacted heart, cancer and stroke legislation and American citizens no longer had to travel to New York or Boston for the finest health care. It would now be available in world-class medical centers across the country, from Seattle to Miami, Los Angeles and Houston to Philadelphia, New Orleans and Chicago.

DOUBLE-EDGED SWORDS

It is imperative that the actions we take to deal with our concerns about the high cost of medical care not destroy the finest health system in the world. It is important to deliver medical diagnosis and treatment at the lowest possible cost. But we must not let our infatuation with managed-care organizations—using the profit motive to make treatment more efficient, downsizing corporations and cutting federal and state budgets—destroy what is good in American health care. For at its best, medical treatment in the United States has no peer.

Managed-care plans are double-edged swords. The smooth edge can cut costs in the delivery of treatment. But the jagged edge can increase bureaucracy and tear at quality, trust and the human touch that have been the defining marks of American health care. Due largely to managed care, in 1997 Americans will spend $200 billion for the paperwork of submitting, reviewing, approving, billing and paying claims. Doctors and nurses must now be masters of the universe of bureaucratic haggling and manipulation as well as masters of medicine.

The pressure for efficiency also leaves physicians little time to talk to patients. If a managed-care physician has 15 minutes to see a patient, what happens at the end of an exam when the patient says to him that her husband is beating her or someone tells him that he's impotent. Medical advice at that point does not fit into a few minutes. We should insist that in the quest for efficiency, we pay doctors for the time they spend talking to patients.

SAFEGUARDING HEALTH CARE QUALITY

Patients, doctors, employers and insurers can all take steps to avert the danger of a decline of quality and trust between doctors and patients. If your doctor doesn't have time to talk to you, fire him and get one who will. Doctors should resist attempts to put profits above patients and efforts to interfere with the doctor-patient relationship or the exercise of their best medical judgment. Employers should provide avenues through which their employees and retirees can complain about reductions in quality of care.

As citizens, we should also keep close tabs on the politicians who want to cut investments in basic biomedical research and support for medical education. We didn't get so many of our best minds into research on cardiovascular disease, cancer, arthritis and AIDS by waving a magic wand. They were attracted by the national, bipartisan commitment to support basic biomedical research and our willingness to recognize the importance of providing reasonable profits to pharmaceutical companies to encourage their investment in applied research to produce, distribute and educate the medical professions about miracle drugs, diagnostic procedures and medical devices.

We should recognize that Medicare is a phenomenal success at providing health care to elderly Americans. There is room for improvement and efficiencies. We can take steps to encourage older Americans to take better care of themselves. For example, Medicare provides free flu vaccinations. Less than 40 percent of eligible individuals take advantage of this Medicare benefit. Why not require those who become ill because they failed to get a flu shot pay the medical expenses for their treatment? Since Medicare beneficiaries who smoke need more medical care than those who don't, why not charge the smokers higher premiums? It might encourage them to quit. It makes more sense to take actions to encourage the elderly to take better care of themselves than to cut the benefits available to them when they get sick.

A SACRED MINISTRY

Most importantly, let each of us insist that our politicians, corporate executives and for-profit health companies accept and act on these fundamental truths: Medicine is a sacred ministry, not an industry. Touching will always be a part of healing. The highest calling of doctors and nurses is to protect and preserve life, heal the sick and comfort the dying. Each of us has a responsibility to pursue healthy lifestyles. If all the actors in the system of American health care live by these basic values, then we can be certain that our grandchildren will live in a nation whose medical treatment remains the envy of the rest of the world.

| "Advanced U.S. medical technology has not translated into better health statistics for its citizens."

AMERICA DOES NOT HAVE THE BEST HEALTH CARE SYSTEM IN THE WORLD

Steve Kangas

In the following viewpoint, Steve Kangas argues that America's health care system fares poorly when compared to those of other industrialized nations. Kangas contends that America's system is the best in the world at treating serious illnesses, but that other nations do a better job of keeping their populations healthy. In his opinion, the United States should provide universal health coverage and more preventive medicine to its citizens. However, he believes the main reasons for Americans' poor health statistics are poverty and income inequality, which he says are linked to poor health. Steve Kangas is a college student living in Santa Cruz, California.

As you read, consider the following questions:

1. In what place does the United States rank in life expectancy when compared to other industrialized nations, according to the statistics cited by the author?
2. Where does Kangas say the United States rank in health care satisfaction, when compared to the 10 largest industrialized nations?
3. What factors contribute to the lower health of the poor, according to Jeffrey Reiman, as quoted by the author?

Adapted from Steve Kangas, "The Long FAQ on Liberalism: Myths About Health Care," web publication at www.scruz.net/~kangaroo/LiberalFAQ.htm. Reprinted with the author's permission.

Myth: The U.S. has the best health care system in the world.

Fact: The U.S. has among the worst health statistics of all rich nations.

The U.S. does not have the best *health care* system in the world—it has the best *emergency care* system in the world. Advanced U.S. medical technology has not translated into better health statistics for its citizens; indeed, the U.S. ranks near the bottom in list after list of international comparisons. Part of the problem is that there is more profit in a pound of cure than an ounce of prevention. Another part of the problem is that America has the highest level of poverty and income inequality among all rich nations, and poverty affects one's health much more than the limited ministrations of a formal health care system.

REVIEWING THE STATISTICS

Let's review the health care statistics first, and analyze them afterwards. All statistics here are for the year 1991; they have generally become worse for the U.S. since then.

Health Care Expenditures (percent of GDP):

United States	**13.4%**
Canada	10.0
Finland	9.1
Sweden	8.6
Germany	8.4
Netherlands	8.4
Norway	7.6
Japan	6.8
United Kingdom	6.6
Denmark	6.5

Percent of population covered by public health care:

ALL NATIONS (except below)	100%
France, Austria	99
Switzerland, Spain, Belgium	98
Germany	92
Netherlands	77
United States	**40**

INDICATORS OF OVERALL HEALTH

Life Expectancy (years):

	Men	Women
Japan	76.2	82.5
France	72.9	81.3
Switzerland	74.1	81.3
Netherlands	73.7	80.5

Sweden	74.2	80.4
Canada	73.4	80.3
Norway	73.1	79.7
Germany	72.6	79.2
Finland	70.7	78.8
United States	**71.6**	**78.6**
United Kingdom	72.7	78.2
Denmark	72.2	77.9

Infant Mortality Rate (per 1,000 live births):

United States	**10.4**
United Kingdom	9.4
Germany	8.5
Denmark	8.1
Canada	7.9
Norway	7.9
Netherlands	7.8
Switzerland	6.8
Finland	5.9
Sweden	5.9
Japan	5.0

Premature Death (years of life lost before the age of 64 per 100 people):

United States	**5.8 years**
Denmark	4.9
Finland	4.8
Canada	4.5
Germany	4.5
United Kingdom	4.4
Norway	4.3
Switzerland	4.1
Netherlands	4.0
Sweden	3.8
Japan	3.3

Percent of people with normal body mass:

	Men	Women
Germany	53%	37%
Finland	51	37
United Kingdom	46	38
Canada	52	29
Switzerland	49	30
France	44	30
Denmark	44	25
United States	**47**	**22**
Sweden	44	25

Percent of people who believe their health care system needs fundamental change:

United States	**60%**
Sweden	58
United Kingdom	52
Japan	47
Netherlands	46
France	42
Canada	38

AN EXPLANATION OF AMERICA'S POOR HEALTH CARE STATISTICS

Sharp readers will notice that the last chart may mean different things to different people. Conservatives think the U.S. health care system needs reform because there is too much government involvement in health care; liberals because there is not enough.

So let's clarify this statistic with a few others. Americans are the most dissatisfied with the quality and quantity of their health care. Of the 10 largest industrialized nations, the U.S. ranked dead last in health care satisfaction, with an approval rating of only 11 percent. There's no putting a positive spin on this statistic; any president with such a low approval rating would be impeached!

Most of this dissatisfaction stems from the high expense and unavailability of U.S. health care. During the 1993 debate on health care reform, polls consistently showed that two-thirds of all Americans supported the idea of universal coverage. Polls also showed that Americans didn't want to pay the higher taxes to achieve this goal, which many pundits took to be an amusing example of public inconsistency. Actually, the public was entirely consistent. Other nations manage to cover everybody, and at lower cost.

Nor is America's international reputation in health care as high as many Americans boast it to be. "Ask anyone you know from a foreign country . . . which country is the envy of the world when it comes to health care," Rush Limbaugh wrote in *See, I Told You So.* But according to a Gallup poll published by the *Toronto Star*, only 2 percent of all Canadians believe that the U.S. has a better health care system than their own.

HEALTH CARE VERSUS EMERGENCY CARE

The fact is that America does not have the finest *health care* system in the world; it has the finest *emergency care* system in the world. Highly trained American doctors can summon Star Wars–type technology in saving patients who have become seriously injured or critically ill. But as far as preventative medicine goes, the U.S. is still in the Stone Age. It should be no surprise that in America's health care *business*, entrepreneurs will take a pound of cure over an ounce of prevention every time.

But in reality, what affects the health of Americans lies more outside the formal health care system than within it. In Europe during the last century, life expectancy nearly doubled after nations purified their drinking water and created sanitation sys-

---

A BIOMEDICAL INDUSTRY, NOT A HEALTH CARE SYSTEM

I don't like the term "health care" for the services provided by the biomedical industry. Resources of the biomedical industry are overwhelmingly allocated to responses to disease, not to the promotion of health. Hence we might say that we have a "disease care" system, but the word "care" is also problematic. The connotations of the word include solicitous regard, compassionate concern, and empathy. . . .

The major incentives seen to be operating within the industry are profit, authority, and prestige, not "care." Hence I refer to the biomedical industry where most others refer to the health care system and I substitute "medical services" for "health care.". . .

There is an analogy often used in public health literature. Suppose there is a steep cliff in the town, and people are falling off. At the bottom of the cliff are all the caring, compassionate people who make up the medical industry. As the people hit the ground, the medical workers rush in to stanch their bleeding, set their fractures, and rush them off to the gleaming new hospital for recovery and rehabilitation.

Meanwhile, at the top of the cliff, there is no warning sign or fence. Indeed, some people are being enticed toward the cliff by people from tobacco and fast food companies and other firms, who are selling them tickets to jump off. Other people are actually in chain gangs, being driven toward the cliff by overseers with whips.

What is the sensible thing to do in this situation? Spend more on the doctors and ambulances and hospitals, so we can get to more of the people faster? Or stop squandering all that money and put up a fence? We do the former because we depend on the market: individuals who have already fallen off the cliff will pay (or their insurers will pay) for treatment; but only society, through its government, will pay to put up a fence, and as a society we have not made this choice.

Bart Laws, *Z Magazine*, July/August 1998.

tems. In America during this century, the highest cancer rates are found in neighborhoods around the chemical industry. A healthy diet and exercise provide better health than most medicines in most circumstances. Other nations have realized that factors outside the hospital are more important than factors inside it, and have used this bit of wisdom to lower their health care costs.

THE LINK BETWEEN POVERTY AND POORER HEALTH

Perhaps the greatest reason why Europeans are healthier than Americans is because they have reduced poverty, especially child poverty. The link between poverty and poorer health has long been proven. One survey reviewed more than 30 other studies on the relationship between class and health, and found that "class influences one's chances of staying alive. Almost without exception, the evidence shows that classes differ on mortality rates." The *American Journal of Epidemiology* states that "a vast body of evidence has shown consistently that those in the lower classes have higher mortality, morbidity and disability rates" and these "are in part due to inadequate medical care services as well as to the impact of a toxic and hazardous physical environment."

And in an even more important finding, studies from Harvard and Berkeley have proven that income *inequality*—not just absolute poverty—is equally important. States with the highest levels of income inequality also have the highest mortality and morbidity rates. The reason why relative poverty matters is because prices and opportunities are relative too—the U.S. may have the best medical technology in the world, but at $10,000 a procedure, who can afford it?

Many reasons contribute to the worse health of the poor. Political scientist Jeffrey Reiman writes: "Less money means less nutritious food, less heat in winter, less fresh air in summer, less distance from sick people, less knowledge about illness or medicine, fewer doctor visits, fewer dental visits, less preventative care, and above all else, less first-quality medical attention when all these other deprivations take their toll and a poor person finds himself seriously ill." And this is not to mention that the poor work and live in more polluted, hazardous and strenuous environments.

TO IMPROVE HEALTH, REDUCE POVERTY

These deprivations are especially hard on infants in their critical development years. The U.S. has tried to combat this problem by offering universal prenatal and postnatal health care, much like Europe does. But the U.S. is fighting against a head wind because it has levels of poverty that Europe does not. Again, a person's health is affected by more factors outside the formal health care system than within it. It's not enough to give a few programs to a person in poverty; what's needed is removing that person from poverty completely.

"When I look back on my years in office," says C. Everett Koop, Reagan's former Surgeon General, "the things I banged my head against were all poverty."

If America is to improve its health statistics, it must not only pass universal health care, but reduce poverty as well.

| "The United States is alone among virtually all industrialized nations in its refusal to recognize health care as a human right."

HEALTH CARE SHOULD BE RECOGNIZED AS A BASIC HUMAN RIGHT

American Medical Student Association

In the following viewpoint, the American Medical Student Association, an activist organization for physicians-in-training, argues that the United States is lagging behind other industrialized nations in recognizing health care as a right. The authors emphasize the number of Americans that lack health insurance, and point out that several other nations provide universal health coverage to their citizens. Most Americans also support universal coverage and health care as a right, says AMSA. The authors conclude that the United States should amend the Constitution to include universal health coverage as an innate human right.

As you read, consider the following questions:

1. What age group does the AMSA describe as most vulnerable to cuts in government and employer-provided health insurance benefits?
2. What three countries do the authors name as examples of nations that have recognized health care as a human right?
3. What does Article 25 of the United Nations' Universal Declaration of Human Rights affirm, according to the authors?

Excerpted from "The United States and the Medically Uninsured: A Crisis of Caring," a web publication by the American Medical Student Association (AMSA) at www.amsa.org/lad/crisis.html. ©1998 by the American Medical Student Association. Reprinted with permission. For the full text of this publication, including references, see the aforementioned website.

O ver the last few decades, the United States has witnessed a steep rise in the number of uninsured citizens. In 1996, more than 17% of Americans lacked any form of health insurance. The problems of the uninsured and underinsured have always plagued the country. However, the situation has drastically worsened within the last decade, claiming record numbers of victims. Solving the uninsured and underinsured problem is indeed a daunting task. However, it's an issue that desperately needs to be addressed.

THE SCOPE OF THE PROBLEM

Middle-class citizens, who rarely worried about health care in the past, suddenly find themselves at the heart of the problem. In the face of rising health-care costs and competition, countless numbers of employers are unable to provide their workers with health insurance. Consequently, more and more employed middle-class Americans find themselves without access to health care.

Adults between the ages of 55 and 64 are perhaps the most vulnerable group. These individuals often find themselves without health insurance as a result of cuts in employer coverage. Although Medicaid provides insurance for those 65 years and older, enrollees often face discrimination and find problems with the quality and accessibility of care. For-profit MCOs (Managed Care Organizations; also known as Health Maintenance Organizations, or HMOs), with their eyes fixed on earnings, have been the worst offenders of slashing care. As the baby-boom generation ages and increasing numbers of elderly citizens require health coverage, Medicare funds are expected to evaporate by 2001.

The Medicaid program fails to cover the majority of those living below the poverty level. Those who do obtain coverage encounter many difficulties. Studies show that Medicaid MCOs have curtailed even basic services. Public hospitals, where many of the Medicaid enrollees obtain care, are being run out of business because of dwindling funds and loss of Medicare/Medicaid revenues to MCOs. As a result, public hospitals have been forced to slam their doors to the poor, who consequently find themselves without health care.

The United States is alone among virtually all industrialized nations in its refusal to recognize health care as a human right. Nations such as Canada, Germany, and the United Kingdom provide universal health coverage to their citizens and receive better patient satisfaction ratings, all at a fraction of the United States' per capita spending on health care. In short, they provide more comprehensive coverage at much lower costs.

It is time for the United States to recognize health care as a basic human right. The American Medical Student Association, in forming Youth for America's Health! (yah!), is taking the first bold step toward addressing our country's health-care injustices. . . .

THE PROBLEM IS WORSENING

History has shown that the economic status of the United States directly impacts the state of health-care delivery. With a booming economy from 1945 to 1970, health-care costs were unchecked and received few criticisms. However, as the United States' economy declined, businesses started to closely examine their finances and raised objections to the rising health-care costs. Employers began to shift the costs of health care to their employees by increasing deductibles and coinsurance payments and enrolling their employees into MCOs.

THE UNIVERSAL DECLARATION OF HUMAN RIGHTS

Article 25.

(1) Everyone has the right to a standard of living adequate for the health and well-being of himself and of his family, including food, clothing, housing and medical care and necessary social services, and the right to security in the event of unemployment, sickness, disability, widowhood, old age or other lack of livelihood in circumstances beyond his control.

(2) Motherhood and childhood are entitled to special care and assistance. All children, whether born in or out of wedlock, shall enjoy the same social protection.

United Nations, 1948.

However, these changes haven't come without criticism. MCOs may have slowed the increasing costs of health care to a degree, but costs are still rising at a rapid rate. In the quest to suppress expenses, insurers have tightly restricted the physician's autonomy in running tests and prescribing treatments, thus interfering with the doctor-patient relationship. The rise of for-profit health care has created an even stronger motive to minimize costs and maximize profits: greed. As a result, physicians find themselves under even stricter regulations and additional pressure to reduce expenditures. Consequently, physicians are influenced by financial considerations when making medical decisions.

As these developments continue, the number of uninsured silently multiply. . . .

THE UNITED STATES STANDS ALONE

Countries spanning the globe regard the United States of America as an esteemed international leader. As the model of democracy and a champion of human rights, it is often the United States that sets the trends and patterns for others to follow. Unfortunately, our country has fallen exceedingly short in providing its citizens with a basic right to health care. For a country whose heritage and inception are based on the beliefs of innate human rights, it is ironic that the United States deprives its citizens of universal health coverage.

The United States is stigmatized as it stands almost alone amongst the industrialized nations of the world in not recognizing health care in its Constitution. Countries such as Canada, the United Kingdom, and Germany have all recognized and hailed health care as a human right and have enacted laws to provide for their citizens accordingly. In doing so, these countries have created health care systems with notably smaller per capita spending coupled with higher satisfaction ratings than the United States. The United Nations, in which the United States serves as an authority figure, created the Universal Declaration of Human Rights which in Article 25 affirms the right to medical care. Clearly, the United States is lagging behind other nations in realizing health care as a right.

AN INNATE HUMAN RIGHT

Universal health coverage has garnered immense public support. Studies have been conducted in 1968, 1975, and 1978 on whether health care should be a privilege or a right. All three polls have produced conclusive results revealing that over 75% of Americans believe that health care should be a right and not a privilege. In a 1986 poll, 86% responded that all Americans should have access to the same quality of health care. Two years later, a Harris poll concluded that 90% believed that everyone should receive health care "as good as a millionaire could get." Public outcry elevated health care as a key issue in the 1992 Presidential Elections. Clearly, the public firmly supports universal health care.

The United States must recognize Universal Health Coverage as a basic human right and amend the Constitution accordingly—for this is not merely the will of the American people, but more significantly, an innate human right.

| "The right to medical care must mean—no exceptions—the power of government, in principle, to determine who gets what."

THERE IS NO RIGHT TO HEALTH CARE

Sheldon Richman

In the following viewpoint, Sheldon Richman argues that the right to medical care is a pseudo-right that would have dangerous implications if it were seriously enforced. There is a limited amount of medical care available, writes Richman; treating health care as a right would give government the power to determine how this limited resource is rationed out. He contends that giving the government such power is tantamount to giving the government control over people's lives. Richman is vice president of policy affairs for the Future of Freedom Foundation, an educational foundation that advocates individual freedom and limited government and opposes socialism and the welfare state.

As you read, consider the following questions:

1. How does Richman describe the principle of nonobligation?
2. In the author's view, what right can the right to medical care not coexist with?
3. What is the worst aspect of a right to medical care, in Richman's opinion?

Reprinted from Sheldon Richman, "The 'Right to Medical Care,'" *The Freeman*, September 1997, by permission of *The Freeman*.

The idea of a right to medical care is so blithely tossed around that most people never take time to ponder the rather serious consequences that would flow from it. It is a classic pseudo-right. A pseudo-right is any claim expressed in rights language that would expand the power of the state at the expense of genuine rights.

The "right to medical care" is seductive. People not accustomed to dissecting political discourse will think of the benefits of having their medical services provided "free" or at a guaranteed affordable price. More sophisticated people may see the proposal as a giant insurance system and feel that there can be no danger in it. If all citizens pay and all have access to care when they need it, what could be wrong?

THE PRINCIPLE OF NONOBLIGATION

Well, a lot could be wrong. Let's start with something basic: for a right to be genuine, it has to be capable of being exercised without anyone's affirmative cooperation. The full exercise of my right of self-ownership requires you to do nothing except refrain from killing or assaulting me. The full exercise of my property rights requires you to do nothing except refrain from taking what is mine. You have no positive, enforceable obligations to me, apart from any you accept through contract.

That principle of nonobligation is an excellent test to which we can submit any proffered right. How does the right to medical care hold up? Leaving out self-treatment, it is difficult to see how there can be such a right. Medical care, unlike air, is not found superabundant in nature. It is produced by someone who spends resources to acquire expertise and education. It requires the use of instruments and drugs, which have to be manufactured by someone. Who is to provide these things? Does the provider have any choice in the matter? What if he refuses? Should he be forced? If so, how shall we distinguish that person from an indentured servant or slave?

Since the "right to medical care" requires an affirmative obligation, it fails the rights test. Put simply, that "right" cannot coexist with the right to be left alone.

Implementation of the "right" does not typically entail forcing doctors, nurses, and manufacturers of medical instruments and pharmaceuticals to provide their services at gunpoint. So what I have said above may not seem germane. But it is, because although providers are not compelled, the taxpayers are. Taxation is somewhat less egregious than conscription, but it is still compulsion. Appropriating people's earnings is tantamount to appropriating their time and labor. Since the compulsion of taxation is spread across large numbers of people, it is less noticeable than the conscription of medical personnel. But it doesn't fundamentally change what's going on.

SCARCITY, "NEED," AND RATIONING

That is only the beginning of what's wrong with trying to enforce a right to medical care. Imagine for a moment a right to apples. That may sound nice, but an immediate problem arises. How many apples? Scarcity is the natural condition, which means that any given moment our wishes exceed the supply of the things we want. (Freedom and free markets have this knack for loosening nature's rather strict bonds of scarcity.) Declaring such a right would be an efficient way of emptying the shelves of apples. And let us ignore the significant question of who would produce apples if we all had a right to them.

We might decide to trust people to take only what they need. But that doesn't get us out of trouble. Even if we assume a population of considerate people, "need," in this context, is a subjective notion. You can probably live without apples; so in one sense, you need none. But if we expand the concept of "need" a little, we open the gates to endless disagreement over who needs how many apples. I may think I need many more than you. There is no way to resolve a dispute of that nature. Well, there is one way: the state can ration apples. We could trust the government to scientifically determine how many apples each of us needs. And if you believe that, you will also believe that the ruling party won't manage to get more apples than the rest of us.

Government control of apples might be no more than an inconvenience. Government control of medical care would be life threatening. Yet what is the alternative once a "right to medical care" is declared? There is no way all people can have all the medical care they wish to have if it is (that is, appears to be) costless. The government will have to decide who gets what. How many of us would take comfort in that?

THE CRUX OF THE ISSUE

Here is the crux of the issue. The right to medical care must mean—no exceptions—the power of government, in principle, to determine who gets what. It may not exercise that power immediately. But given the economics of the matter, it will, sooner or later. I submit that this has nothing to do with rights and everything to do with control, literally, of people's lives.

I do not exaggerate. A major ethical issue these days involves the "right to die," or the right to assisted suicide. That is over-shadowing one that may be more consequential, the so-called "duty to die." Some years ago, then-Colorado Governor Richard Lamm argued that old people should know when it is time to quit this earth in favor of younger people. (The civil libertarian Nat Hentoff wrote recently that Lamm is, inexplicably, a devotee of exercise.) John Hardwig, a medical ethicist and social philosopher, has now picked up the cause of the duty to die. He writes that medical advances and an "individualist culture" may have many people believing that "they have a right to medical care and a right to live, despite the burdens and costs to our families and society." He adds that "there may be a fairly common responsibility to end one's life in the absence of any terminal illness . . . a duty to die even when one would prefer to live."

HEALTH CARE ENCOMPASSES MANY CONTROVERSIAL ISSUES

The provision of health care as a basic uniform civil right is more intrusive than any other element of the welfare state: health care dramatically touches all the important passages of life, from reproduction and birth to suffering and death. The commitment to a particular package of services brings with it a particular interpretation of the significance of reproduction, birth, health, suffering, death, and equality (e.g., it involves specific positions regarding artificial insemination by donors, prenatal diagnosis with the possibility of selective abortion, physician-assisted suicide, voluntary active euthanasia, and unequal access to better basic health care). A uniform welfare right to health care involves endorsing and establishing one among a number of competing concrete moralities of life, death, and equality. Because of this tie to morally controversial interventions, the establishment of uniform, universal health-care welfare rights directly or indirectly involves citizens, patients, physicians, nurses, and others in receiving or providing health care in a health-care system which they may find morally opprobrious.

H. Tristram Engelhardt Jr., *Social Philosophy & Policy*, Summer 1997.

For our purposes we need not address whether an old person should preserve his heirs' inheritance rather than spend it on medical care. At the moment, that is a private, not a political, matter of how one spends one's own money. (The inheritance tax could have consequences for such a decision.) What is relevant is how that ethical issue is transformed when government controls medical spending via "the right to health care." The Lamm-Hardwig line would be translated into a rather unpleasant public policy: the withholding of care for the elderly in the name of "making room" for the young. The government giveth rights; the government taketh them away. As a matter of public policy, might not the politicians and bureaucrats decide that heart transplants, knee replacements, and mastectomies for octogenarians are a waste of money? This sort of thing is not considered beyond the pale in the increasingly fragile welfare states of western Europe.

IF GOVERNMENT CONTROLS MEDICAL SPENDING, IT CONTROLS YOU

All of this is a rather roundabout way of identifying the worst aspect of the "right to medical care": the tethering of the citizen to the state. For all the criticism that is leveled at Medicare and proposals to reform medical care in general, too little attention has gone to that uncomfortable fact. If government controls medical spending, it controls you, including the very length of your life.

We may correlate the progress of mankind with the extent of its independence from the state. To put it mildly, national health insurance would be a setback.

Yet that is the direction in which we move. New regulations governing the portability of insurance policies and coverage of existing conditions all portend creeping comprehensive control. The newest cause, uninsured children, does the same. Ludwig von Mises explained why in his *Critique of Interventionism*. One regulation creates problems, which are used to justify the next intervention. For example, if Congress says mental-health benefits have to be equal to medical benefits, the cost of insurance will go up. That will then be the excuse to force young people who don't wish to pay those premiums to buy insurance. Next on the agenda will be price controls on doctors and insurance companies. When companies flee the straitjacketed market, the government will step in. This is not conspiracy. It's logic.

It all starts with an innocuous phrase, the right to medical care. Language is a potent thing. Let us handle it with care.

| "[The growing number of uninsured]
is the biggest problem we face in
American health care."

THE UNINSURED ARE A SERIOUS PROBLEM

Robert Pear

In the following viewpoint, Robert Pear, a reporter for the *New York Times*, describes how the number of Americans without health insurance continues to rise despite government efforts to expand coverage. The main problem, the author explains, is the cost of health insurance: More employers offer health insurance than in the 1980s, but fewer workers choose to pay the increasingly high premiums. Federal lawmakers have proposed several reforms to expand health insurance coverage, but few have garnered major support because, the author reports, there is disagreement over whether employers should be required to provide health insurance and concern that new laws would further raise health insurance premiums.

As you read, consider the following questions:

1. What fraction of the population lacks health insurance, according to Pear?
2. In the author's opinion, how has the attitude of the middle class toward the plight of the uninsured changed since the early 1990s?
3. What two groups does the Federal Agency for Health Care Policy and Research say are becoming more likely to decline employer-sponsored health insurance?

In 1994, when President Clinton's effort to reshape the American health care system collapsed, a political consensus emerged from the rubble: in the future, any such changes should be made piecemeal, one step at a time.

THE NUMBER OF UNINSURED CONTINUES TO GROW

But four years later, the limits of that incremental approach are becoming clear, in the view of many experts. Most immediately, Congress is confronting demands to provide broad new consumer protections for patients fed up with the restrictions of managed care. Lawmakers also face a deeper, more intractable problem. Despite the passage of several laws intended to expand coverage step by step, the number of Americans without insurance has risen steadily, by an average of one million a year.

The number of uninsured has increased each year since 1987 and, in 1998, now exceeds 41 million, roughly one-sixth of the population.

Moreover, this steady rise has occurred despite a remarkable economic boom. The nation has created more than 14 million jobs since 1993, but most of these are in small businesses, which are far less likely to provide health insurance than are large companies.

In Congress, members of both parties keep returning to the problems of the uninsured, but the cost and complexity of the issue pose extraordinary hurdles. Lawmakers say they are determined not to repeat the mistakes that killed Mr. Clinton's plan, but beyond that, there is little agreement.

Congress has enacted two significant health care laws since the collapse of the Clinton plan. It created a new program to finance health care for low-income children in 1997. And in 1996 it passed the Kassebaum-Kennedy law, to make insurance more readily available to millions of people who change their jobs or lose them.

These efforts, along with previous expansions of the Medicaid program, have made a difference; without them, experts say, the number of uninsured would be even higher. . . .

A PATCHWORK SYSTEM FOR THE UNINSURED

[However,] neither the new laws nor the power of a fiercely competitive medical marketplace has delivered health insurance to Mildred Davis, a custodian and security guard in Austin, Tex.

"I have no health insurance, no dental plan," Ms. Davis said as she sat at the front desk of the community health center where she works. "When you walk into a doctor's office, the first thing they say is: 'How will you pay? What insurance do you have?' I have to go to the bank before I go to the doctor."

Like many people who are uninsured, she deferred doctors' visits and medical care until she had a serious need.

As a result, said Ms. Davis, who is 48, she had an emergency hysterectomy in January 1998 after several weeks of uterine bleeding. She received a hospital bill for $8,000 and a doctor's bill for $2,000.

"I would have gotten care earlier if I had had health insurance," she said. Instead, she waited until the pain became unbearable.

"I would get up to patrol this area," Ms. Davis said, pointing to the corridors of the health center. "The pain was so bad that I'd fall over. I lost four and a half pints of blood. I was literally bleeding to death."

Ms. Davis's case highlights the patchwork nature of the current insurance system and illustrates what can happen to uninsured people when they become ill. Even if parents have coverage through their employers, their children may be uninsured. (Many companies have cut back benefits for dependents.) Conversely, many children covered by Medicaid, the Federal-state program for low-income people, have parents who are uninsured because Medicaid's eligibility rules are much more generous for children than they are for adults.

SLIPPING THROUGH THE CRACKS

Ms. Davis said that her 7-year-old daughter was covered by Medicaid. But Ms. Davis herself, like many of the uninsured, was caught in between. Her income was too high for her to qualify for Medicaid, and she could not afford private insurance. Ms. Davis says she hopes to get health insurance later this year when she becomes a full-time city employee.

The Medicaid eligibility rules are devilishly complex. They differ from state to state, and family income limits vary with a child's age. So a healthy 4-year-old boy may be protected by Medicaid, while his 8-year-old sister, though severely ill, is ineligible for coverage because the income limit for her age group is lower.

The plight of the uninsured may seem distant to members of the middle class riding the current economic boom. People are less anxious about losing their jobs and their benefits than they were in the recession of the early 1990's. "Health security" was the buzzword then, just as "patients' rights" is now.

But William S. Custer, an economist at Georgia State University in Atlanta, said: "The problems that the Clinton health plan was intended to address have not gone away and may worsen in the future. If the economy slows or if health costs rise much faster than prices in general, we'll probably see more rapid growth in the number of Americans without health insurance."

OPTING FOR PAY OVER INSURANCE

Today, as in the early 1990's, the cost of coverage is crucial. Paradoxically, the Public Health Service says, the number of workers offered health insurance by their employers has increased in the last decade, but the proportion of workers who accept such offers has declined, in part because of the cost.

Philip F. Cooper and Barbara S. Schone, economists at the Federal Agency for Health Care Policy and Research, found large declines in the proportion of people accepting employer-sponsored insurance among two groups: workers with low wages (less than $7 an hour) and workers younger than 25.

They estimate that six million workers are offered health insurance by their employers or their unions but do not take it.

Rita J. Carrillo, 26, works 30 to 40 hours a week as a customer service representative for a company that schedules repairs for Frigidaire appliances in Texas. The company offers health insurance, she said, but "for me as a single mother, it's too expensive to afford."

Ms. Carrillo explained: "My paycheck after taxes is $350 to $400 every two weeks. For health insurance, they would deduct $60 from each paycheck. I would be left with $290, which is not a lot to deal with. If I could afford the insurance, I would take the children to the doctor more often. Lucky for me, they are healthy children."

Nationwide, about half of all uninsured workers are either self-employed or working in businesses that have fewer than 25 employees. When coverage is available in such companies, the employees are often required to pay a large share of the cost.

Small businesses give many reasons for not providing insurance to their employees. They say that premiums are too high, that their profits are too uncertain for them to make a commitment to insurance and that health benefits are not always a high priority for workers.

Sal Z. Valiani, who operates four dry-cleaning shops in Austin, said that he offered health insurance long ago and even paid half the cost. But, he said, employees repeatedly asked him not to deduct their share of the premiums from their wages.

"It's one or the other, a pay raise or health benefits," Mr. Valiani said, and in the eyes of many employees, higher wages are considered more important. . . .

No Consensus on How to Proceed

Lawmakers say they keep looking for ways to expand coverage, but there are sharp divisions over how to do it. Republicans are philosophically opposed to price controls, which play a role in some schemes to expand coverage, and few Democrats openly advocate such regulation. Some liberal Democrats continue to push legislation that would require employers to provide coverage, but such mandates are anathema to conservatives in both parties.

Federal lawmakers in general are reluctant to dictate programs to the states. And they say they cannot find the money for the subsidies that would be needed to make insurance truly affordable to millions of low-income Americans. As a result, the plight of the uninsured appears to be a low political priority in the current Congress, much to the frustration of their advocates.

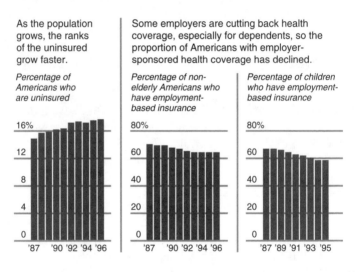

The Growing Ranks Without Coverage

As the population grows, the ranks of the uninsured grow faster.

Percentage of Americans who are uninsured

Some employers are cutting back health coverage, especially for dependents, so the proportion of Americans with employer-sponsored health coverage has declined.

Percentage of non-elderly Americans who have employment-based insurance

Percentage of children who have employment-based insurance

Sources: The Kaiser Commission on Medicaid and the Uninsured; Census Bureau.

Senator Paul Wellstone, Democrat of Minnesota and a potential Presidential contender, says: "Here we are at peak economic performance, and we are being told that we cannot provide health coverage for everyone. If not now, when?"

Representative Bill Archer, the Texas Republican who is chairman of the House Ways and Means Committee, and Senator William V. Roth Jr., the Delaware Republican who is chairman of the Senate Finance Committee, want to create tax breaks to help people buy private insurance. Representative Thomas J. Bliley Jr., the Virginia Republican who is chairman of the Commerce Committee, wants to create "health marts" to offer insurance to self-employed people and businesses with fewer than 500 employees.

Senator Kennedy has introduced a bill that would require employers with 50 or more employees to offer insurance to their workers and to pay at least 72 percent of the premiums.

"Every business is expected to pay a minimum wage and to obey the child labor laws," Mr. Kennedy said. "It is long past time for businesses to contribute to the cost of basic health insurance coverage for their workers. There can be no excuse for large firms to shirk their responsibility."

And Senator Wellstone recently introduced a bill that would give states large sums of Federal money to help achieve the goal of universal insurance coverage.

Proposals like those from Mr. Kennedy and Mr. Wellstone stir little interest in a Congress controlled by Republicans, who are viscerally opposed to any new mandates on employers.

Republicans say such mandates will not work in a voluntary employer-sponsored health insurance system. There is, they say, strong evidence that employers will drop coverage (especially for workers' dependents), curtail benefits or shift costs to employees if the Government imposes new requirements. And in interviews, uninsured workers say that, while they yearn for coverage, they are very sensitive to the cost. They often pass up the offer of health insurance if it will take a noticeable amount from their paychecks.

A Major Problem, But Not on the Political Agenda

But concern for the uninsured will not die. The Health Insurance Association of America, which helped kill President Clinton's proposals with its "Harry and Louise" commercials in 1994, is now seeking ways to extend private coverage to the uninsured.

"Newspapers, television and radio news reports may no longer focus on the plight of the uninsured as they did in 1993 and 1994," said Donald M. Peterson, who is chairman of the association and of the Trustmark Insurance Company in Lake Forest, Ill. "But for millions of Americans, the lack of affordable coverage remains a crisis."

Insurers worry that if the erosion of private employer-sponsored insurance continues, consumers will demand new Government programs, to which the industry is opposed.

Drew E. Altman, president of the Henry J. Kaiser Family Foundation, which has done many studies of the uninsured, said: "This is the biggest problem we face in American health care, and it's not on the political agenda. There's no significant solution on the horizon. The country doesn't want to put up the tens of billions of dollars it would take to provide coverage for the uninsured. We have been making some progress with the small incremental reforms, but it's like shoveling sand against the tide."

"[The rise of health-care costs], far from being a symptom of modern medicine's failure, is a product of its success."

ADVANCES IN MEDICINE HAVE CAUSED A HEALTH CARE CRISIS

Willard Gaylin

Modern medicine has become too expensive for everyone to have unlimited access to health care, argues Willard Gaylin in the following viewpoint. Gaylin, a professor of psychiatry at Columbia University Medical School and president of the Hastings Center for bioethical research in Briarcliff Manor, New York, maintains that the number of treatments and ailments encompassed by the term "health care" has grown continuously since the late 19th century. In Gaylin's opinion, the cost of health care will continue to rise because medicine will be able to accomplish more each year. Since, in his view, the cost of comprehensive health care cannot be reduced, Gaylin concludes that health care must be rationed.

As you read, consider the following questions:

1. In the author's view, how were impaired eyesight, hearing, potency, and fertility once understood, and how are they thought of today?
2. In Gaylin's view, how do most American men define "death with dignity"?
3. According to Gaylin, by how much have health care costs in the United States risen in the past 25 years, as a percent of the gross domestic product?

Excerpted from Willard Gaylin, "Health Unlimited," *The Wilson Quarterly*, Summer 1996. Reprinted by permission of the author.

The debate over the current crisis in health care often seems to swirl like a dust storm, generating little but further obfuscation as it drearily goes around and around. And no wonder. Attempts to explain how we got into this mess—and it is a mess—seem invariably to begin in precisely the wrong place. Most experts have been focusing on the failures and deficiencies of modern medicine. The litany is familiar: greedy physicians, unnecessary procedures, expensive technologies, and so on. Each of these certainly adds its pennyweight to the scales. But even were we to make angels out of doctors and philanthropists out of insurance company executives, we would not stem the rise of health-care costs. That is because this increase, far from being a symptom of modern medicine's failure, is a product of its success.

Good medicine keeps sick people alive. It increases the percentage of people in the population with illnesses. The fact that there are proportionally more people with arteriosclerotic heart disease, diabetes, essential hypertension, and other chronic—and expensive—diseases in the United States than there are in Iraq, Nigeria, or Colombia paradoxically signals the triumph of the American health-care system.

EXPANDING THE DEFINITION OF HEALTH

There is another and perhaps even more important way in which modern medicine keeps costs rising: by altering our very definition of sickness and vastly expanding the boundaries of what is considered the domain of health care. This process is not entirely new. Consider this example. As I am writing now, I am using reading glasses, prescribed on the basis of an ophthalmologist's diagnosis of presbyopia, a loss of acuity in close-range vision. Before the invention of the glass lens, there was no such disease as presbyopia. It simply was expected that old people wouldn't be able to read without difficulty, if indeed they could read at all. Declining eyesight, like diminished hearing, potency, and fertility, was regarded as an inevitable part of growing older. But once impairments are no longer perceived as inevitable, they become curable impediments to healthy functioning—illnesses in need of treatment.

To understand how the domain of health care has expanded, one must go back to the late 19th century, when modern medicine was born in the laboratories of Europe—mainly those of France and Germany. Through the genius of researchers such as Wilhelm Wundt, Rudolph Virchow, Robert Koch, and Louis Pasteur, a basic understanding of human physiology was established, the foundations of pathology were laid, and the first true understanding of the nature of disease—the germ theory—was developed. Researchers and physicians now had a much better understanding of what was going on in the human body, but there was still little they could do about it. As late as 1950, a distinguished physiologist could tell an incoming class of medical students that, until then, medical intervention had taken more lives than it had saved.

THE MIRACLES OF MODERN MEDICINE

Even as this truth was being articulated, however, a second revolution in medicine was under way. It was only after breakthroughs in the late 1930s and during World War II that the age of therapeutic medicine began to emerge. With the discovery of the sulfonamides, and then of penicillin and a series of major antibiotics, medicine finally became what the laity in its ignorance had always assumed it to be: a lifesaving enterprise. We in the medical profession became very effective at treating sick people and saving lives—so effective, in fact, that until the advent of AIDS (acquired immune deficiency syndrome), we arrogantly assumed that we had conquered infectious diseases.

The control of infection and the development of new anesthetics permitted extraordinary medical interventions that previously had been inconceivable. As a result, the traditional quantitative methods of evaluating alternative procedures became outmoded. "Survival days," for example, was traditionally the one central measurement by which various treatments for a cancer were weighed. If one treatment averaged 100 survival days and another averaged 50 survival days, then the first treatment was considered, if not twice as good, at least superior. But today, the new antibiotics permit surgical procedures so extravagant and extreme that the old standard no longer makes sense. An oncologist once made this point using an example that remains indelibly imprinted on my mind: 100 days of survival without a face, he observed, may not be superior to 50 days of survival with a face.

QUALITY OF LIFE AS A MEDICAL ISSUE

Introducing considerations of the nature or quality of survival adds a whole new dimension to the definitions of sickness and health. Increasingly, to be "healthy," one must not only be free of disease but enjoy a good "quality of life." Happiness, self-fulfillment, and enrichment have been added to the criteria for medical treatment. This has set the stage for a profound expansion of the concept of health and a changed perception of the ends of medicine. . . .

Until recently, for example, infertility was not considered a disease. It was a God-given condition. With the advances in modern medicine—in vitro fertilization, artificial insemination, and surrogate mothering—a whole new array of cures was discovered for "illnesses" that had to be invented. And this, of course, meant new demands for dollars to be spent on health care.

Unnecessary Expenditures

One might question the necessity of some of these expenditures. Many knee operations, for instance, are performed so that the individual can continue to play golf or to ski, and many elbow operations are done for tennis buffs. Are these things for which anyone other than the amateur athlete himself should pay? If a person is free of pain except when playing tennis, should not the only insurable prescription be—much as the old joke has it—to stop playing tennis? How much "quality of life" is an American entitled to have?

New technologies also exert strong pressure to expand the domain of health. Consider the seemingly rather undramatic development of the electronic fetal monitor. It used to be that when a pregnant woman in labor came to a hospital—if she came at all—she was "observed" by a nurse, who at frequent intervals checked the fetal heartbeat with a stethoscope. If it became more rapid, suggesting fetal distress, a Caesarean section was considered. But once the electronic fetal monitor came into common use in the 1970s, continuous monitoring by the device became standard. As a result, there was a huge increase in the number of Caesareans performed in major teaching hospitals across the country, to the point that 30 to 32 percent of the pregnant women in those hospitals were giving birth through surgery. It is ridiculous to suggest that one out of three pregnancies requires surgical intervention. Yet technology, or rather the seductiveness of technology, has caused that to happen.

The American Character

Linked to the national enthusiasm for high technology is the archetypically American reluctance to acknowledge that there are limits, not just limits to health care but limits to anything. The American character is different. Why this is so was suggested some years ago by historian William Leuchtenberg in a lecture on the meaning of the frontier. To Europeans, he explained, the frontier meant limits. You sowed seed up to the border and then you had to stop; you cut timber up to the border and then you had to stop; you journeyed across your country to the border and then you had to stop. In America, the frontier had exactly the opposite connotation: it was where things began. If you ran out of timber, you went to the frontier, where there was more; if you ran out of land, again, you went to the frontier for more. Whatever it was that you ran out of, you would find more if you kept pushing forward. That is our historical experience, and it is a key to the American character. We simply refuse to accept limits. Why should the provision of health care be an exception?

RISING HEALTH-CARE COSTS

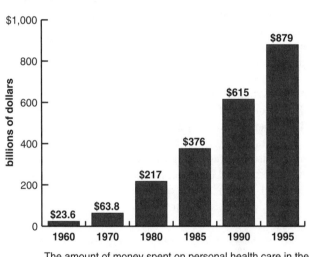

The amount of money spent on personal health care in the U.S. has risen sharply over the past 35 years. In 1995, total health-care expenditures were about $879 billion, an amount equal to about 13% of all economic activity in the U.S.

Source: Health Care Financing Administration

To see that it isn't, all one need do is consider Americans' infatuation with such notions as "death with dignity," which translates into death without dying, and "growing old gracefully," which on close inspection turns out to mean living a long time without aging. The only "death with dignity" that most American men seem willing to accept is to die in one's sleep at the age of 92 after winning three sets of tennis from one's 40-year-old grandson in the afternoon and making passionate love to one's wife twice in the evening. This does indeed sound like a wonderful way to go—but it may not be entirely realistic to think that that is what lies in store for most of us.

HEALTH CARE MUST BE RATIONED

During the past 25 years, health-care costs in the United States have risen from six percent of the gross national product to about 14 percent. If spending continues on its current trajectory, it will bankrupt the country. To my knowledge, there is no way to alter that trajectory except by limiting access to health care and by limiting the incessant expansion of the concept of health. There is absolutely no evidence that the costs of health-care services can be brought under control through improved management techniques alone. So-called managed care saves money, for the most part, by offering less—by covert allocation. Expensive, unprofitable operations such as burn centers, neonatal intensive care units, and emergency rooms are curtailed or eliminated (with the comforting, if perhaps unrealistic, thought that municipal and university hospitals will make up the difference).

Rationing, when done, should not be hidden; nor should it be left to the discretion of a relative handful of health-care managers. It requires open discussion and wide participation. When that which we are rationing is life itself, the decisions as to how, what, and when must be made by a consensus of the public at large through its elected and other representatives, in open debate. . . .

The painful but necessary decisions involved in explicit rationing are, obviously, not just medical matters—and they must not be left to physicians or health-care managers. Nor should they be left to philosophers designated as "bioethicists," though these may be helpful. The population at large will have to reach a consensus, through the messy—but noble—devices of democratic government. This will require legislation, as well as litigation and case law.

In the late 1980s, the state of Oregon began to face up to the necessity of rationing. The state legislature decided to extend Medicaid coverage to more poor people but to pay for the change by curbing Medicaid costs by explicitly rationing benefits. (Eventually, rationing was to be extended to virtually all Oregonians, but that part of the plan later ran afoul of federal regulations.) After hundreds of public hearings, a priority list of services was drawn up to guide the allocation of funds. As a result, dozens of services became difficult (but not impossible) for the poor to obtain through Medicaid. These range from psychotherapy for sexual dysfunctions and severe conduct disorder to medical therapy for chronic bronchitis and splints for TMJ Disorder, a painful jaw condition. Although the idea of explicit rationing created a furor at first, most Oregonians came to accept it. Most other Americans will have to do the same.

ACCEPTING LIMITS

Our nation has a health-care crisis, and rationing is the only solution. There is no honorable way that we Americans can duck this responsibility. Despite our historical reluctance to accept limits, we must finally acknowledge that they exist, in health care, as in life itself.

"If we are going to solve America's
health care problems, we need to
understand them. Otherwise, we will
be throwing money and programs at
problems that really do not exist."

THE PROBLEMS OF THE HEALTH CARE
SYSTEM ARE EXAGGERATED

Merrill Matthews Jr. and John C. Goodman

In the following viewpoint, Merrill Matthews Jr. and John C.
Goodman argue that many criticisms of the U.S. health care system are exaggerated or unfounded. For example, they contend
that Americans' relatively poor health statistics can be explained
by differences in the ethnic makeup of U.S. and European populations. The authors argue that more emphasis on preventive
medicine would not reduce healthcare inflation. Finally, they
claim that the problem of the uninsured is not as bad as most
estimates suggest. Goodman and Matthews are president and
vice president of domestic policy, respectively, of the National
Center for Policy Analysis, a public policy research institute with
headquarters in Dallas.

As you read, consider the following questions:
1. According to the authors, what are some factors that have a
   greater effect on life expectancy than does medical care?
2. In Matthews and Goodman's view, what is the effect of
   preventive medicine on health care costs?
3. What fraction of uninsured spells end within twelve months,
   according to the authors?

Excerpted from Merrill Matthews Jr. and John C. Goodman, "Myths About Our Health
Care System: Lessons for Policy Makers," *The St. Croix Review*, August 1995. Reprinted by
permission of the authors.

Critics of the American health care system have propagated a number of myths to justify greater government control over our health care system. This viewpoint identifies [some] of the most common myths and exposes the fictions that underlie each. This article was prepared by the National Center for Policy Analysis.

MYTHS ABOUT HEALTH CARE QUALITY

Myth: Life expectancy is a good indicator of health care quality.

If you needed heart surgery, would you prefer to have the surgery done in Cuba, Barbados, Costa Rica, or the United States?

Some people take life expectancy as a key indicator of the quality of a country's health care system. If they are right, you should be indifferent to whether your surgery is performed in Cuba or the United States, since the two have the same life expectancy, 75.6 years. And you would have to conclude that the health care system in Barbados (75.3 years) is almost the same. In fact, if you took general life expectancy as your guide, you might choose Costa Rica, since life expectancy there (76 years) is higher than in the United States.

Sounds silly? Of course it does. While a good health care system may extend the life of a small percentage of a population, the quality of health care people receive has only marginal impact on the average life span of the population as a whole. Life expectancy in all but the least-developed countries is primarily a result of lifestyle, environment, education, and other genetic and social factors rather than the quality of medical care.

For example, Japan's average life expectancy (78.6 years) is one of the highest in the world, about three years higher than the United States. If the three-year difference were the result of lower-quality U.S. care, Japanese-Americans living in this country should experience shortened life spans. They don't.

- According to the National Asian Pacific Center on Aging, in 1980 (the latest comparison numbers available) white Americans had an average life expectancy of 76.4 years, while Japanese-Americans had an average life expectancy of 79.7 years—about the same three-year spread that exists between the populations of the two countries.
- Similarly, the California Department of Health reports that people of Asian or Pacific-Island ethnic origin living in the state have a life expectancy 5.3 years longer (81.2 vs. 75.9) than white Californians.

Claiming that the American health care system is inferior to the health care systems of countries with longer life expectancies is like comparing apples and oranges. Nearly all of the industrialized countries with better life expectancies than the United States, except Japan, have overwhelmingly white populations of European descent. None have large black populations. Unfortunately, black Americans have more health problems and shorter life expectancy (70 years in 1991) than whites. The American population is a mixture of ethnic groups—some with longer and some with shorter life spans than European whites.

When comparing ethnic groups across national borders, the U.S. statistics appear much more favorable. For example, life expectancy for male Indians in Canada is 63.4 years vs. 67.1 years for male American Indians. Among females the contrast is even greater, 68.9 years in Canada vs. 78.1 years in the United States.

Myth: Low infant mortality is a good indicator of quality.

Some maintain that a low infant mortality rate indicates that a health care system provides easy access to prenatal care. However, the evidence shows that differences in infant mortality more frequently reflect differences in parental lifestyle, environment, and genetic endowments than in access to quality medical care.

- Data from the California Department of Health Services, for example, show the average infant mortality rate was 8.6 deaths per 1,000 live births in 1989.
- But Americans of Japanese descent living in California had an infant mortality rate of 4.8 deaths per 1,000 live births in 1989 (the latest data available for this population).
- The Chinese had 7.1 deaths, Filipinos 7.8 deaths, Hispanics 7.8 deaths, whites 7.7 deaths, and blacks, 18.0 deaths per 1,000 live births.

Since individuals in the different groups often live in the same communities and use the same hospitals and physicians, the difference in infant mortality rates cannot be attributed to the health care system.

Critics of U.S. health care often claim that infant mortality rates among minorities would be lower if we had a single-payer system similar to that of Canada. Yet in Canada the nationwide infant mortality rate is twice as high for Indians as for non-Indians, while the Indian infant mortality rate in the United States is slightly lower than that for non-Indians.

SHORTER HOSPITAL STAYS ARE A SIGN OF EFFICIENCY

Myth: Time spent in hospitals is a good measure of the quality of care.

Some also claim that more hospital admissions and longer stays indicate better care. By this standard, the United States rates poorly.

- The average hospital stay was only 9.1 days in the United States in 1990, compared to an average of 15.7 days in all developed countries.
- In Japan, the average length of a hospital stay is fifty days, *more than eight times that of the United States.*
- Only three Organization for Economic Cooperation and Development (OECD) countries—Denmark (8.0), Ireland (8.0), and Turkey (6.9)—have shorter average stays than the U.S.

Far from being a problem, less inpatient and more outpatient care has been a *goal* of U.S. health care policy for the past two decades. And—other things equal—most health economists regard shorter stays as a sign of hospital efficiency, not of the failure to provide needed care. . . .

Myth: *Preventive care saves money.*

A common complaint about our health care system is that people do not get enough preventive care, including prenatal care, immunizations, mammograms, and physical checkups.

Most Uninsured Spells Are Brief

Who's uninsured? A big problem in discussing health insurance coverage is the use of the Census Bureau's calculation of the uninsured. Typically, these figures represent a snapshot—how many are uninsured at any given time. What they ignore is the fact that many people who lose insurance coverage get it back again relatively quickly. Often, that's because they are between jobs, or starting with a company that imposes a waiting period before coverage kicks in, or work for a firm that doesn't offer health benefits, and so on. These transitional periods are far less worrisome than chronic lack of insurance coverage—that is, going without coverage for many years.

The Census Bureau estimates that about 13.8% of children under age 18 lacked insurance coverage in 1995—that's about 9.8 million kids. . . .

How long do these children go without coverage? As it turns out, Census conducts a separate analysis that tracks people's coverage over a span of 28 months, breaking the numbers down by age group.

According to that analysis, children under 18 years old tend to go without coverage for relatively short periods of time. Of the 68 million children in the country, about 70% were continuously covered for the entire 28 months. Only a tiny fraction—4%—went without for the entire 28 months. Half of those children who lost coverage got it back again in nine months or less.

John Merline, *Consumers' Research Magazine*, June 1997.

Many argue that expanded preventive care would save health care dollars by preempting more costly acute care. For example, whereas prenatal care costs only a couple of hundred dollars, medical care for a premature baby usually costs nearly $20,000 more than a normal birth. And whereas vaccinations for measles, mumps, and rubella cost about $20 each, the average hospital cost to treat those diseases is about $21,000.

On the theory that preventive care for all children and pregnant women would *save* money over time, many health care reform proposals include such services as free prenatal care, immunizations, and well-baby care. But whether such proposals would expand access to care or save money is doubtful.

Does free care increase access? Although nationally only a little more than half of all children are immunized by the age of two, more than 95 percent are fully immunized by age five so they can enter school. Is the difference between the vaccination rate at ages two and five primarily due to the barrier of price? The evidence suggests otherwise.

Take Massachusetts, which has the nation's oldest free immunization program. Vaccinations there are available to all children without charge, regardless of the parents' financial means. Are all Massachusetts's children immunized? Hardly.

- While the national average is about 58 percent of children properly immunized by the age of two, in Massachusetts the rate is 62 percent.
- In the 11 other states with free childhood immunization programs, the rates are only marginally better.

PREVENTIVE MEDICINE RAISES HEALTH CARE COSTS

Many contend that the cost of prenatal care is more than offset by a reduction in the number of premature and low birth weight babies, whose medical costs can be astronomical. Papers in scholarly journals have even specified savings from prenatal care. For every $1.00 spent, one paper said the savings would be $1.70, another said $2.57 and a third $3.38. However, a review of more than 100 such papers reveals:

- Only a dozen papers made specific claims about the cost savings of prenatal care—and serious flaws in the methodology of all twelve made their findings questionable.
- Most of the other papers reviewed cited one or more of the twelve flawed papers as their proof that prenatal care pays off.

Careful studies show that, in general, preventive medicine raises rather than lowers overall health care costs. Although prenatal care is important, preventive medicine is "economical" only when special at-risk groups are targeted. Preventive service for the entire population usually costs more than it saves.

This does not mean that preventive care is wasteful. Diagnostic tests often relieve patients' anxiety and reassures them of good health. Thus, for the most part, preventive care is like a consumer good that creates benefits in return for a cost. It is not like an investment good that delivers a positive rate of economic return.

THE MYTH OF THE UNINSURED

Myth: Being uninsured is a chronic problem.

The latest estimates suggest that at any one time 40 million Americans are uninsured. And during the course of a year 58 million are uninsured for at least one month. However, most uninsured spells are temporary, half last less than six months and nearly three-fourths end within 12 months. Ultimately, only 18 percent of all uninsured spells last for more than two years. Most of the temporarily uninsured will, by definition, become insured eventually without changes in government policy. At the moment, the majority choose not to purchase private insurance because they judge its cost too high relative to its benefits. But many become insured after a change of jobs allows them to obtain insurance subsidized by employers and by government.

However, some individuals *are* chronically uninsured. Besides the long-term unemployed, they include drug dealers, prostitutes, others who work in the underground economy and people who are transient and homeless.

Being uninsured, then, is similar to being unemployed. The vast majority of people experience both conditions at some time in their lives, but very few stay uninsured or unemployed for long periods.

Myth: Preexisting conditions prevent a large number of people from obtaining health insurance.

Sick people who lose their health insurance may find it impossible to purchase new coverage. Insurers may classify them as uninsurable, offer them a policy that excluded their preexisting conditions or set their risk-rated premiums unaffordably high.

How big is this problem? Not very big. According to the Agency for Health Care Policy and Research, a branch of the U.S. Public Health Service, only 0.7 percent of the U.S. population (about two million people) has been denied health insurance due to a medical condition. And while we do not know how many people pay excessive health insurance premiums, it cannot be very many. Only about 3 percent of the population say they are in fair or poor health. . . .

THE NEED TO DISPEL HEALTH CARE MYTHS

If we are going to solve America's health care problems, we need to understand them. Otherwise, we will be throwing money and programs at problems that really do not exist. But understanding our health care problems means eliminating some of the myths that surround the health care debate. Reforms targeted at vulnerable populations will do a better job than huge bureaucratic programs of getting care to those in need.

PERIODICAL BIBLIOGRAPHY

The following articles have been selected to supplement the diverse views presented in this chapter. Addresses are provided for periodicals not indexed in the *Readers' Guide to Periodical Literature*, the *Alternative Press Index*, the *Social Sciences Index*, or the *Index to Legal Periodicals and Books*.

Clement Bezold	"Your Health in 2010: Four Scenarios," *Futurist*, September/October 1996.
Henry M. Greenberg	"American Medicine Is on the Right Track," *Journal of the American Medical Association*, February 11, 1998. Available from PO Box 10945, Chicago, IL 60610.
Jacob S. Hacker	"National Health Care Reform: An Idea Whose Time Came and Went," *Journal of Health Politics, Policy, and Law*, Winter 1996. Available from Duke University Press, 905 W. Main St., 18-B, Durham, NC 27701.
John Hood	"The Profit Motive for High-Tech Healing," *Policy Review*, November/December 1997.
John K. Iglehart	"The American Health Care System— Expenditures," first of an eight-part series, *New England Journal of Medicine*, January 7, 1999. Available from 10 Shattuck St., Boston, MA 02115-6094 or http://www.nejm.org.
Ruth Larson	"Wealth, Education Help Americans Live Longer," *Insight*, August 31, 1998. Available from 3600 New York Ave. NE, Washington, DC 20001.
Charles F. Longino Jr.	"Myths of an Aging America," *American Demographics*, August 1994.
Andrew Phillips	"Faltering Reform: The Number of Uninsured Americans Is Growing," *Maclean's*, December 2, 1996.
Robert J. Samuelson	"Having It All: Americans Want the Impossible When It Comes to Health Care," *Newsweek*, September 28, 1998.
Paul Starr	"What Happened to Health Care Reform?" *American Prospect*, Winter 1995.
Wilson Quarterly	"Healing American Health Care," special section, Summer 1996.

How Has Managed Care Affected the Health Care System?

CHAPTER PREFACE

"Managed care" is a term used to describe several types of health insurance plans which are designed to reduce health care costs. Health maintenance organizations (HMOs) are the most common type of managed care plan, and are popular because they offer lower premiums, copayments, and deductibles than do most traditional health plans.

In principle, managed care seeks to keep health care costs down by keeping patients healthy. To this end, managed care plans make preventive medicine such as vaccines, mammograms, and cholesterol tests very inexpensive. HMOs also reduce costs by limiting patients' access to expensive specialists and procedures. Each patient chooses a primary care physician from the HMO's network of doctors, and must get this doctor's approval for all exams, procedures, hospital visits, and referrals to medical specialists.

Supporters of managed care believe this system benefits patients because it eliminates expensive, unnecessary care. Robert J. Samuelson, a contributing editor of *Newsweek*, believes managed care is controversial because "it challenges the idea that more health care is always better." HMOs provide only medically necessary care, he says, in contrast to traditional fee-for-service health plans in which doctors are paid for each service they perform, and thus have a financial incentive to prescribe unnecessary tests and medical procedures.

However, critics believe that HMO doctors may have a financial incentive to provide too little care. For example, one method that some HMOs use to pay doctors is called capitation: Doctors receive a fixed monthly sum with which to treat their patients, and whatever the doctors don't use, they keep. Critics also charge that HMOs financially reward doctors who cut costs and refuse to contract with doctors who prescribe too many expensive services.

Because of these management practices, the main targets of managed care's opponents are not doctors, but rather the managed care executives pressuring them to cut costs. In fact, few critics dispute the basic principle of managed care, which is that health care should be cost-efficient. Instead, they charge that corporations have abused the system, denying care wherever they can in order to increase profits. In his book *The Medical Racket*, author Martin L. Gross claims that "The HMO is not a medical plan at all, but strictly an insurance gimmick."

Managed care is a method of keeping health care costs down. The authors in the following chapter will discuss whether it has been successful in doing so, and whether it has done so at the expense of health care quality.

| "The rise of managed care was a historically necessary response to a crisis facing the nation's health care system."

MANAGED CARE IS NECESSARY TO CONTROL HEALTH CARE COSTS

Susan Brink

In the following viewpoint, Susan Brink, a senior writer for *U.S. News & World Report*, argues that the shift to managed care has saved the United States billions of dollars in health care spending, an accomplishment that she believes the critics of managed care often overlook. Managed care's emphasis on cost control is so beneficial, says Brink, because under the fee-for-service model of medicine health care spending was spiraling out of control and increasingly large numbers of people were unable to afford health insurance. The author concludes that although the health care industry still faces many challenges, on the whole managed care represents an improvement in the way Americans receive health care.

As you read, consider the following questions:

1. In Brink's opinion, what was the major problem with the fee-for-service model of health care?
2. According to Brink, how many Americans who are insured through their employers belong to a managed care plan?
3. How did hospitals pay for the health care needs of uninsured people under the fee-for-service health care system, according to the author?

Reprinted from Susan Brink, "HMOs Were the Right Rx," *U.S. News & World Report*, March 9, 1998, with permission. Copyright 1998, U.S. News & World Report.

Helen Hunt, as a single mother with a sickly child in the movie *As Good As It Gets*, spews out an obscenity-laced denunciation of her HMO for caring more about money than about her son's health. In some movie theaters, her diatribe elicits cheers from the audience.

It's no surprise. Three in four Americans are worried about their health care coverage, according to a survey by *U.S. News & World Report* and the Kaiser Family Foundation (not associated with Kaiser Permanente HMOs). One in six respondents has experienced delays in getting appointments. One fourth can't figure out their medical bills, and 1 in 5 has had problems paying them. Half of the respondents say they're worried that doctors are basing treatment decisions strictly on what the health plan will cover.

In short, America's health care system has become hard to live with. Many believe HMOs are to blame. But living without them may be impossible. The mounting complaints about HMOs have tended to obscure the genuine gains that have occurred in the managed-care era—for patients, for companies, for the overall economy. Thanks to managed care, most Americans have more money in their pockets and may also be healthier. Thanks to managed care, more companies can afford to provide health benefits to employees. For most Americans, however, the new system's achievements have remained largely invisible—in contrast to the highly visible indignities and inconveniences it sometimes imposes on them.

UNBEARABLE INFLATION

The biggest achievement by far has been controlling runaway costs. Under the old system, inflation in health care costs weakened the entire American economy, boosting the price of every product and handicapping U.S. firms relative to competitors overseas. These problems were the paradoxical side effect of the great achievements in public health in the 20th century.

During the so-called golden age of medical science following World War II, new drugs and equipment helped increase the average life span of Americans from 63 years in 1940 to 76 years in 1996. Under the "fee for service" model that preceded the age of managed care, doctors and hospitals had a financial incentive to throw everything they could at every malady. The more procedures they carried out, the more income they earned. Because "third-party payment" insurance systems were prevalent before managed care, patients had the same incentive. They passed their bills straight to the insurer and had little reason to economize. Medicare became law in 1965, further institutional-izing a "blank check" mentality under which the government and private insurers were expected to pay most or all of virtually any bill submitted.

The result was extraordinary health care inflation. In 1980, Americans spent $247 billion on health care, or 8.9 percent of the gross domestic product. Ten years later, that figure was $697 billion—an alarming 12.1 percent of GDP. Projections by the Congressional Budget Office into the early years of the next century put health care costs as high as 16 percent of GDP (by comparison, Japan spends 7.2 percent and Canada spends 9.6). "No private insurance company ever said no to any bill ever shoved under its nose," says Uwe Reinhardt, professor of economics at Princeton University. With outlays rising so fast, something had to give—and it did, as copayments went up and standard benefits were reduced.

MANAGED CARE SAYS NO

Managed care said no—and meant it. In 1995, Americans spent $988 billion (or 13.6 percent of GDP) on health care—which was a lot, but significantly less than the $1.07 trillion, or 14.8 percent of GDP, that the Congressional Budget Office had fore-cast only three years earlier. The savings were largely due to managed care.

In 1997, the American Association of Health Plans, an industry trade organization, released a report by the Lewin Group claim-ing credit for between $116 billion and $181 billion in health care savings from 1990 to 1996. If employers passed those sav-ings on to workers, the average worker could gain an extra $228 in yearly take-home pay ($408 for the average married couple, $191 for the average single person). States with more wide-spread managed care, like California, where 37 percent of people belong to an HMO, saved even more—$770 per family.

General Motors, the largest private-sector purchaser of health care, has held the line on health spending for the past three or four years, largely because of managed care. Unfortunately for GM, holding the line still means spending a staggering $4.8 bil-lion a year, or $1,200 for every vehicle GM builds. But without managed care, the burden would be even greater.

Not surprisingly, U.S. corporations have become the most ar-dent fans of managed care. "We were spending all this money, and we had no idea whether that meant we had a healthier, more productive work force," said Sherrie Matza, vice president of corporate human resources at Bank of America. Like a growing number of large corporations, Bank of America began steering employees into lower-cost managed-care policies at the start of the decade. Three years later, the bank estimated that it had saved nearly 40 percent compared with fee-for-service plans. (In 1993, Arizona estimated that it had saved 40 percent on Medicaid costs through managed care.) All told, U.S. employers in 1996 saved an average of 11 percent on managed-care plans compared with old-style indemnity plans. Today, about 3 out of 4 Americans insured through their employers belong to some kind of managed-care plan.

Still, few Americans seem to have connected these savings with HMOs or managed care. "Flat premiums meant your paycheck was bigger. But the average employee doesn't think that that $116 billion had anything to do with their paycheck," says Princeton's Reinhardt.

BETTER HEALTH CARE RESULTS

There is also solid evidence that, contrary to Helen Hunt's on-screen complaints, managed care brings better health care results than does fee for service. A study in the September 24, 1997 *Journal of the American Medical Association* found, for example, that older patients suffered through fewer episodes of "potentially ineffective care," hospital jargon for care that prolongs an inevitable death. Treatment in the last six months of life for those over 65 accounts for 21 percent of all Medicare spending. And the care is often futile, painful, degrading—even unwanted. The study showed that HMO patients were 25 percent less likely to suffer through such care.

Managed care also seems to do a better job of finding some cancers—breast, cervical, colon, and melanoma—sooner than fee-for-service plans, according to a study in the *American Journal of Public Health*. And in the lucrative and highly competitive field of open heart surgery, California managed-care plans were found to steer patients to facilities that do a high volume of cases, according to the *Health Affairs* journal. High-volume facilities, studies show, have fewer deaths and lower costs. "There's no question in my mind that because of managed care, fewer people are dying of inappropriate surgery," says Michael Millenson, consultant with William M. Mercer and author of *Demanding Medical Excellence: Doctors and Accountability in the Information Age*. "The problem with all of these people who are not being killed is that very few people know it. Your doctor doesn't say, 'You know, I was going to recommend inappropriate surgery, but because of managed care, I won't.'"

Rising Costs and the Uninsured Remain Problems

For all its achievements, the managed-care industry faces formidable challenges. Like a recurring cancer, health care inflation, apparently vanquished, is returning. Rising costs are eating into HMO profits in ways even expanding membership can't offset. Kaiser Permanente, the most venerable representative of the managed-care movement, reported a record $270 million loss for 1997—despite increasing its membership by 19 percent. And Oxford Health Plans reported a fourth-quarter loss of more than $200 million. Once the darling of investors, Oxford saw a more than 60 percent drop in its stock price last fall.

As a result, employers are bracing for another round of premium increases. After four years of stable or declining premium rates for federal employees, the 1998 rates will rise 8.5 percent, according to the Office of Personnel Management. Neil Howe, an economist affiliated with the Concord Coalition, a nonpartisan deficit-fighting group, notes that the managed-care revolution has achieved genuine one-time cost savings, but "all the underlying cost drivers—from aging to technology to rising expectations—are again kicking in."

Keeping Health Care Affordable

The old system being replaced—call it unmanaged care—had failed the nation in two crucial respects: It was both unaccountable and unaffordable. . . .

One of the reasons why more than 40 million Americans are uninsured is because so many employers were pushed to the wall by health costs bearing little relationship to the quality and effectiveness of care.

Eventually someone had to accept responsibility for bringing this situation under control. The United States has rejected the notion of putting the government in charge of health care. Instead, thousands of managed-care organizations abiding by numerous public- and private-sector regulations have taken up the challenge of delivering care that meets consistently high standards of quality and consumer satisfaction while protecting purchasers against being blindsided by hit-and-run costs.

This transition didn't happen by accident, and it's working. Researchers have estimated, for example, that 5 million Americans who have health coverage today under managed care would have been priced out of the market by now under the old system. That's 5 million reasons to take note of the progress that has been made.

Karen Ignagni, *Insight*, June 22, 1998.

Now that its successes have made it a permanent feature of American medicine, managed care will be asked to face additional challenges. How does it restrain the theoretically limitless demand for medical services without the arbitrary rules that made crowds cheer for Helen Hunt? How does it provide what is not purely a commercial service—the preservation of life and health—through an increasingly for-profit model? How does it allow for the tens of millions of Americans who have no insurance? The old system covered poor people through a hidden tax on employers and the insured population. Because no one was insisting that bills reflect actual care given, hospitals could send out bills designed to cover overall costs. A few aspirin, for example, might be billed at $20. The hospital could "cost-shift" that income to pay for people who showed up with no money and no insurance.

With the managed-care revolution of the 1990s, insurers began negotiating fees. They insisted that they pay only for the actual care provided to their insured patients. The poor and uninsured still show up, creating financial strains on hospitals that cannot morally—or legally—turn them away. While hospital administrators insist the squeeze has not affected the quality of care, others point to reductions in nursing staff and hospital comforts as a consequence.

It's also true that managed-care companies have a high percentage of young, healthy customers. This is attractive as a business model, but it is at odds with the demographic trends of a country whose average age is rising. The demand for medical care inevitably rises with age. As a result, the financial pressures facing HMOs will only get worse, says Arthur Caplan, director of the Center for Bioethics at the University of Pennsylvania: "What we think we're in now with cost containment and rationing is nothing compared to when the boomers age."

HERE TO STAY

The rise of managed care was a historically necessary response to a crisis facing the nation's health care system. Coping with the next set of challenges won't be easy. Improving the managed-care system is essential; dismantling it is unrealistic. Norman Rockwell's corner doctor is gone for good.

"160.3 million of us now find ourselves held captive to corporate health-care systems that earn $952 billion a year but can't afford the luxury of a conscience or a heart."

MANAGED CARE IS UNETHICAL

Ronald J. Glasser

Ronald J. Glasser argues in the following viewpoint that managed care is an unethical scheme designed to make money rather than to help the sick or injured. Because a managed care organization's profits are the difference between what its members pay for insurance and what the company spends on treating them, says Glasser, the most profitable managed care organizations are the ones that spend the least on patient care. The author maintains that this framework is in conflict with physicians' moral obligations to their patients; in his opinion, the principles of for-profit health care violate medical ethics. Glasser is a pediatrician and the author of several books, including *The Light in the Skull: An Odyssey of Medical Discovery*.

As you read, consider the following questions:

1. In Glasser's view, how is the practice of providing health care only to people who are already employed a form of "cherry picking"?
2. How does the author define "medical-loss ratio"?
3. How much did the average executive of a managed care company make in 1996, according to the author?

We are born, we live, and then we die, but these days we do so with less and less help from a medical profession paid to discount our suffering and ignore our pain. Proofs of the bitter joke implicit in the phrase "managed care" show up in every morning's newspaper, in casual conversations with relatives or friends recently returned from a hospital or from what was once thought of as a doctor's office instead of an insurance company's waiting room, and in a country generously supplied with competent and compassionate doctors, 160.3 million of us now find ourselves held captive to corporate health-care systems that earn $952 billion a year but can't afford the luxury of a conscience or a heart.

A BROAD REMOVAL OF HEALTH-CARE BENEFITS

Childless women in every city in America dread the simplest fertility workups because they know that the evaluation probably will serve as evidence denying them future payments for diseases of the vagina, uterus, or ovaries; the rest of us have had our co-payments increased, our use of prescription drugs curtailed or replaced by corporate-sanctioned medications, stays in the hospital reduced or eliminated, "pre-authorizations" required for necessary and routine tests. The broad removal of health-care benefits takes place at all points of the country's medical-industrial complex, and in line with the tone and temper of the times more than 2,300 Massachusetts physicians in December of 1997 signed a despairing manifesto in the *Journal of the American Medical Association*:

> The time we are allowed to spend with the sick shrinks under the pressure to increase throughput, as though we were dealing with industrial commodities rather than afflicted human beings. . . . Physicians and nurses are being prodded by threats and bribes to abdicate allegiance to patients, and to shun the sickest, who may be unprofitable. Some of us risk being fired or "delisted" for giving, or even discussing, expensive services, and many are offered bonuses for minimizing care.

Such forced denial of care occurs at a time when new medical and surgical technologies allow physicians to treat and often cure any number of conditions that only a few years ago barely could be diagnosed. . . .

But although a good many of us suspect that somehow we are being swindled, and those of us who have fallen seriously ill know for a fact that the purveyors of managed care often wish we would go away or die—as quietly and quickly as possible—we're reluctant to draw the commercial moral of the tale.

The system wasn't meant to care for sick people; it was meant to make and manage money.

THE VIRUS OF THE PROFIT MOTIVE

The theory of "managed care" first attracted attention in the 1940s in the coal regions of Kentucky and West Virginia. Labor unions hired doctors, constructed clinics and hospitals, and supplied prepaid medical services at a fixed monthly rate to their members and their families. The fixed rate per patient was unrelated to the patient's use of the service. By the 1950s, a few large companies had taken a similarly paternalistic stance and were offering contract health care to their own employees. The arrangement was not designed to profit anyone other than those who received care, which was why it worked.

But in the 1970s, the government and large corporate employers began to seek ways to reduce health-care costs, and the concept of contract medicine was injected with the virus of the profit motive. Cadres of systems managers . . . brought forth new corporate structures meant to introduce market forces into the industry and named by the several acronyms (HMO, PPO, POS, etc.) for preferred or managed medicine. Not only were a lot of people going to get well, but some of them were going to get rich. First promoted by what is known as InterStudy (a health-policy think tank organized in 1972), the proposition relied on the idea that an HMO could make money if it provided medical care only to people who enjoyed the prior benefits of perfect health and a full-time job. Thus the practice known as "cherry picking," which virtually removed the burden of insuring people who were seriously ill. You simply cannot be employed full time if you suffer from the effects of a crippling disability or disease.

The full story of how and why, over the short span of twenty years, the concept of the HMO came to dominate nearly every phase of American medicine (directing the distribution of every operation, wheelchair, test, and pill) would embrace all the arts of financial chicanery made popular in the 1980s. . . . Here was but one scheme in an era of schemes, the HMO as a brilliant means of redistributing income from individual physicians to corporate executives and shareholders. The short-term profits were extraordinary: PacifiCare, for example, swelled from a $168,911 enterprise in 1986 to a $10 billion behemoth by 1997.

For corporations and small businesses burdened with rising medical costs, the HMO appeared as a gift from heaven. As recently as 1980 company health plans enrolled only a small percentage of the eligible employees; in 1997 the plans enrolled 85 percent, up from 48 percent in 1993. The percentage of doctors practicing outside the HMOs meanwhile has dwindled to the present 19.9 percent.

A Ponzi Scheme

But the spectacular success of managed care proved to be the cause of its equally spectacular failures. Cherry picking is another name for a Ponzi scheme [an investment swindle in which some early investors are paid off with money put up by later ones in order to encourage more and bigger risks], and sooner or later it falls apart. Even a company blessed with tens of thousands of healthy subscribers eventually finds itself obliged to pay for the occasional premature birth at $1,500 a day, or the occasional employee who develops a brain tumor or whose wife is diagnosed with ovarian cancer. There are car accidents and near drownings. There are the late complications of diabetes, the forty-year-old struck down with a heart attack, the previously undiagnosed melanoma, the complications of hypertension. . . .

When a company finds itself hard-pressed for profit, then behind the closed doors of the executive suite what has been left unsaid becomes the loud and forthright voice of reason: *Yes, we are a company that cares about the well-being of the American people, but the free market is the free market, and so* . . . And so, among the middle managers and accountants of the nation's health plans the talk these days turns to ways of lowering what Wall Street calls an HMO's "medical-loss ratio"—i.e., that percentage of yearly revenues allotted to patient care. The term, in and of itself, repudiates every principle that undergirds the profession of medicine and flatly contradicts the Hippocratic oath, which pledges a physician's first responsibility to the care of his or her patient. But banks don't accept payment in oaths, as was made plain by an analyst from Nutmeg Securities, Ira Zuckerman, who reminded his prospective investors that the attractiveness of managed-care companies as investments changes when health plans sign up members who will actually have to see a doctor. The rule of thumb holds that a managed-care business is in trouble if more than 65 percent of its enrollees submit a significant claim in any one-year period. Little wonder then that rehabilitation for stroke victims or occupational therapy for spinal-cord injuries no longer make the list of benefits. Managed-care companies actually seek to hide their competencies; no HMO wishes to advertise its successes with cystic fibrosis or multiple sclerosis, or, say, the skill of its subspecialists who treat AIDS. Were a company to become known for treating complicated or expensive diseases, it would run the real risk of attracting the attention of the very sick. The blurring of priorities becomes embarrassingly obvious in the newspaper ads that promote the virtues of the country's prepaid health plans. As, for instance, in the December 1997 *Minneapolis Star Tribune*:

> We offer an extensive and unique program of reporting quality, accessibility and satisfaction data to consumers at the clinic and physician level—through the internet and other mechanisms.

> We developed a doctor-led organization, called the Institute for Clinical Systems Integration, that develops nationally recognized medical best practices using the best medical minds in our community.

> We have received numerous national awards for our community health improvement initiatives.

> We created the nation's first comprehensive program to encourage reading and brain stimulation for infants and young children.

MANAGED CARE'S FAIRY TALES

Managed care has managed to eliminate from the public-policy debate any and all words that describe suffering and disease, and together with the good news about "reporting quality," and "satisfaction data," the industry defends itself against past, present, and future criticism by explaining the symptoms that afflict the country's health-care system with warm and welcome fairy tales that the public apparently still chooses to believe:

All doctors are rich and omnipotent: The stereotyped image of the aloof and wealthy physician driving a Mercedes or wandering over a golf course allows the proponents of managed care to imply, usually with a good deal of success, that any doctor who speaks ill of corporatized medicine is, by definition, a greedy and callous fellow who thinks only about his fees.

As a percentage of all medical costs, the money allotted to physicians' services has remained constant over the last thirty years. Between 1993 and 1995, what the American Medical Association calls "median physician net income (after expenses, before taxes)" declined, in real terms, by 1.4 percent. Surgeons and radiologists, among them the most highly paid practitioners in any of the medical professions, earned, on average in 1995, roughly $250,000. The sums dwindle into pittances when compared with the earnings of the executives of publicly traded managed-care companies, which, on average in 1996, approached the handsome sum of $10 million. What inflates the price of medicine in the United States is the cost of corporate vice presidents, not the cost of doctors. . . .

THE MYTH OF UNNECESSARY, OVERLY EXPENSIVE CARE

The patient loves going to the hospital: As corollary to the story of the rich doctor, the health-care companies tell the story of the patient as spendthrift fool, who, if left to his or her own devices, will bankrupt the country with an "infinite demand" for heart transplants, kidney dialysis, and liposuction. But as with the health-care industry's other probings of imaginary symptoms, the diagnosis has been proven false. Most people check into hospitals only when they have no choice in the matter, and the nonexistent phenomenon of infinite demand doesn't lead to the unproven result of infinite cost. New medical treatments and surgical procedures, no matter how expensive when first introduced, retain their original costly forms for astonishingly short periods. Less expensive and less complicated therapies invariably replace the early experiments.

The evolving art of kidney dialysis offers the textbook case in point. Long before the advent of managed care, kidney specialists looking for an alternative to hemodialysis—with its inconvenience, risks of infection, clotting, and blood loss, as well as its complicated machinery—pursued the development of the less demanding peritoneal dialysis. So also with balloon angioplasty, which today has become the preferred alternative to the expensive coronary bypass. So also with every other specialty that anybody but an insurance agent cares to name.

An axiom of economics holds that nothing can be rationed that is itself not scarce, and, absent evidence of infinite demand and infinite cost, you can't ration health care when there are more than enough doctors, hospitals, and high-tech equipment distributed through the country to do everything and anything that needs to be done. American health care is an unsaturated demand market, and in such markets "rationing" is simply a code word for not spending the money to take care of the poor, the uninsured, the underinsured, and the high-risk patient.

BLAMING THE PATIENT

Sickness is the patient's fault, and death is a preventable disease: Because we live in a society that equates youth and wellness with intelligence and superior moral character, the health-care industry can pretend that it really isn't supposed to do anything at all. If the patient hadn't been so careless—if he or she had given up smoking and drinking, read the complete works of [alternative medicine guru] Andrew

Weil, cut down on the day's fat intake, checked the blood pressure, ridden the stationary bicycle, ingested the correct amounts of garlic and zinc, gotten in touch with the inner child—then the patient wouldn't be making so many awful noises, wouldn't be conspiring to harm the "medical-loss ratio," wouldn't be bothering doctors (busy and important people, albeit overpaid) with the miserable proofs of their weakness and stupidity. . . .

Reprinted by permission of Harley Schwadron.

In truth, it is a dangerous world out there. Slip through the ice, get hit on the freeway, wake up with blood in your urine, have trouble breathing, stumble about after a splitting headache, lose the ability to feel, have trouble remembering things, experience ringing in your ears, find mucus in your stools, start gasping at night, and garlic pills will be of little help. But wellness is the panacea of the 1990s, and the health plans promote the wonders of aerobic exercise and fat-free diets in order to obscure the real purpose of medicine, which is the treatment of illness and the relief of suffering. To the extent that the plans can shift the burden of health care to the private sectors of personal hygiene and morality, they excuse themselves from the tedious and increasingly expensive chores of providing a public service or addressing the common good.

CARING FOR MONEY INSTEAD OF PEOPLE

For the last twenty years the theory and practice of managed care has enjoyed the protection of the political and financial interests—insurance companies, the pharmaceutical industry, large business corporations, suppliers of hospital equipment, members of Congress—eager to keep the Ponzi scheme profitably in place. Assured of the approval of the best people that money can buy, the HMOs have gone calmly about the business of eliminating one treatment after another and adding one doctor after the next to their rosters. . . .

[The] health-care industry [is] sickened with the virus of "medical-loss ratio" and unlikely to recover until cured of its addiction to the profit motive. A physician is not by nature a commodities broker, a clinic is not a meat-packing plant, and unless the health-care industry quits caring for money instead of people, its chronic pathology almost certainly will be referred to the consulting rooms of government. Not that the politicians will want to take the case, but let enough people make strong enough complaint, and the therapeutics committees in the country's legislatures might be forced to write a new and not so mean-spirited set of guidelines.

"If patients knew how much clinical authority was actually stripped from their doctors in managed care plans, they might be more reluctant to join."

MANAGED CARE HAS HARMED THE HEALTH CARE SYSTEM

Deborah A. Stone

In the following viewpoint, Deborah A. Stone argues that the quality of care that managed care organizations provide is severely hampered by such organizations' need to maximize profits. Stone contends that managed care plans dictate to doctors what services they can and cannot offer, and give financial bonuses to doctors who skimp on care. Under managed care, she writes, doctors are encouraged to worry about money rather than the welfare of their patients, and are rewarded for avoiding sick patients rather than treating them. Stone is a professor of politics and social policy at Radcliffe College.

As you read, consider the following questions:

1. In 1957, what did the American Medical Association doctors first forbid doctors to do, according to Stone?
2. Why did physician David Blumenthal receive a $1,200 check from his HMO, as quoted by the author?
3. What types of misleading statements do HMOs often make in their brochures, according to Stone?

Excerpted from Deborah A. Stone, "Bedside Manna: Medicine Turned Upside Down," *The American Prospect*, vol. 31, March/April 1997. Reprinted by permission of *The American Prospect*. Copyright 1997 The American Prospect, PO Box 383080, Cambridge, MA 02138. All rights reserved.

For more than 150 years, American medicine aspired to an ethical ideal of the separation of money from medical care. Medical practice was a money-making proposition, to be sure, and doctors were entrepreneurs as well as healers. But the lodestar that guided professional calling and evoked public trust was the idea that at the bedside, clinical judgment should be untainted by financial considerations.

Although medicine never quite lived up to that ideal, the new regime of managed care health insurance is an epic reversal of the principle. Today, insurers deliberately try to influence doctors' clinical decisions with money—either the prospect of more of it or the threat of less. What's even more astounding is that this manipulation of medical judgment by money is no longer seen in policy circles as a corruption of science or a betrayal of the doctor-patient relationship. Profit-driven medical decisionmaking is extolled as the path to social responsibility, efficient use of resources, and even medical excellence. . . .

MONEY AND MEDICINE

Before the mid-nineteenth century, the business relationship between doctors and patients was simple: The patient paid money in exchange for the doctor's advice, skill, and medicines. However, to win acceptance as professionals and be perceived as something more than commercial salesmen, doctors needed to persuade the public that they were acting out of knowledge and altruism rather than self-interest and profit. Organized medicine built a system of formal education, examinations, licensing, and professional discipline, all meant to assure that doctors' recommendations were based on medical science and the needs of the patient, rather than profit seeking.

In theory, this system eliminated commercial motivation from medicine by selecting high-minded students, acculturating them during medical training, and enforcing a code of ethics that put patients' interests first. In practice, medicine remained substantially a business, and no one behaved more like an economic cartel than the American Medical Association. The system of credentialing doctors eventually eliminated most alternative healers and, by limiting the supply of doctors, enhanced the profitability of doctoring. Nonetheless, medical leaders espoused the ideal and justified these and other market restrictions as necessary to protect patients' health, not doctors' incomes.

It took the growth of health insurance to create a system in which a doctor truly did not need to consider patients' financial means in weighing their clinical needs, so long as the patient was insured. As Columbia University historian David Rothman has shown, private health insurance was advertised to the American middle class on the promise that it would neutralize financial considerations when people needed medical care. Blue Cross ads hinted darkly that health insurance meant not being treated like a poor person—not having to use the public hospital and not suffering the indignity of a ward. Quality of medical care, the ads screamed between the lines, was indeed connected to money, but health insurance could sever the connection.

By 1957, the AMA's Principles of Medical Ethics forbade a doctor to "dispose of his services under terms or conditions that tend to interfere with or impair the free and complete exercise of his medical judgment or skill. . . ." This statement was the apotheosis of the ethical ideal of separating clinical judgment from money. It symbolized the long struggle to make doctoring a scientific and humane calling rather than a commercial enterprise, at least in the public's eyes if not always in actual fact. But the AMA never acknowledged that fee-for-service payment, the dominant arrangement and the only payment method it approved at the time, might itself "interfere with" medical judgment. . . .

THE NEED TO KEEP DOWN COSTS

Sooner or later, the ideal of medical practice untainted by financial concerns had to clash with economic reality. Everything that goes into medical care is a resource with a cost, and people's decisions about using resources are always at least partly influenced by cost. By the 1970s, with health care spending hitting 9 percent of the gross national product (GNP) and costs for taxpayers and employers skyrocketing, America perceived itself to be in a medical cost crisis. Doctors and hospitals, however, resisted cost control measures. By the late 1980s, neither the medical profession, the hospitals, the insurers, nor the government had managed to reconcile the traditional fee-for-service system with cost control, even though the number of people without health insurance grew steadily.

During these decades, a pervasive antigovernment sentiment and a resurgence of laissez-faire capitalism on the intellectual right combined to push the United States toward market solutions to its cost crisis. Other countries with universal public-private health insurance systems have watched their spending rise, too, driven by the same underlying forces of demographics and technology. But unlike the U.S., they rely on organized cooperation and planning to contain costs rather than on influencing individual doctors with financial punishment or reward.

Some national health systems pay each doctor a flat salary, which eliminates the financial incentive to over-treat, though it might create a mild incentive to under-treat. Systems with more nearly universal health insurance schemes also eliminate expensive competition between insurers, because there is no outlay for risk selection, marketing, or case-by-case pretreatment approval, and far less administrative expense generally. . . .

The distinctive feature of the emerging American way of cost control is our reliance on market competition and personal economic incentive to govern the system. For the most part, such incentives are contrived by insurers. In practice, that has meant insurers have far more power in our system than in any other, and it has meant that they insert financial considerations into medical care at a level of detail and personal control unimaginable in any other country. . . .

MANAGED CARE REWARDS DOCTORS FOR DOING LESS

Today, financial incentives on doctors are reversed. Instead of the general incentives of fee-for-service medicine to perform more services and procedures, contractual arrangements between payers and doctors now exert financial pressures to do less. These pressures affect every aspect of the doctor-patient relationship: how doctors and patients choose each other, how many patients a doctor accepts, how much time he or she spends with them, what diagnostic tests the doctor orders, what referrals the doctor makes, what procedures to perform, which of several potentially beneficial therapies to administer, which of several potentially effective drugs to prescribe, whether to hospitalize a patient, when to discharge a patient, and when to give up on a patient with severe illness. . . .

Studies of HMOs by Alan Hillman of the University of Pennsylvania found that two-thirds of HMOs routinely withhold a part of each primary care doctor's pay. Of the plans that withhold, about a third withhold less than 10 percent of the doctor's pay and almost half withhold between 11 and 20 percent. A few withhold even more. These "withholds" are the real financial stick of managed care, because doctors are told they may eventually receive all, part, or none of their withheld pay. In some HMOs, the rebate a doctor receives depends solely on his or her own behavior—whether he or she sent too many patients to specialists, ordered too many tests, or had too many patients in the hospital. In other plans, each doctor's rebate is tied to the performance of a larger group of doctors. In either case, doctors are vividly aware that a significant portion of their pay is tied to their willingness to hold down the care they dole out. . . .

Of course, not all HMOs provide financial incentives that reward doctors for denying necessary care. In principle, consumers could punish managed care plans that restricted clinical freedoms, and doctors could refuse to work for them. But as insurers merge and a few gain control of large market shares, and as one or two HMOs come to dominate a local market, doctors and patients may not have much choice about which ones to join. The theorists' safeguards may prove largely theoretical.

THE MIRAGE OF SATISFACTION

You'd think patients prevented from obtaining the services they want (whether or not they are the services they need) would complain. Yet the 1994 Federal Employee Health Benefits Program showed that 86% of HMO members were satisfied with managed care—a satisfaction rate higher than [fee-for-service] has.

To account for this, you have to realize the most HMO members in any given year are not patients. Studies that survey all HMO members rather than only those who become patients are biased toward satisfaction.

By way of analogy, imagine a comparison between two health clubs. The first—the Health Club Maintenance Organization—costs nothing up front, and claims everything is provided. The second—a Fee-for-Service Health club—requires you to pay a small amount every time you attend, and makes no grandiose claims. Now poll the people in the two clubs, keeping in mind that 95% of the members never attend either club. Even if the 5% who actually use the clubs prefer the Fee-for-Service club (because of the shorter wait to use its equipment, the larger supply of new equipment, and the greater ease in scheduling a visit with a trainer), their opinions will be drowned out by a poll of all members.

Ross Levatter and Jeffrey A. Singer, *Liberty*, November 1996.

In the early managed-market theory of economist Alain Enthoven and others, the doctor was supposed to make clinical decisions on the basis of cost-effectiveness analysis. That would mean considering the probability of "success" of procedure, the cost of care for each patient, and the benefit to society of spending resources for this treatment on this patient compared to spending them in some other way. But in the new managed care payment systems, financial incentives do not push doctors to think primarily about cost-effectiveness but rather to think about the effect of costs on their own income. Instead of asking themselves whether a procedure is medically necessary for a patient or cost-effective for society, they are led to ask whether it is financially tolerable for themselves. Conscientious doctors may well try to use their knowledge of cost-effectiveness studies to help them make the difficult rationing decisions they are forced to make, but the financial incentives built into managed care do not in themselves encourage anything but personal income maximization. Ironically, managed care returns doctors to the role of salesmen—but now they are rewarded for selling fewer services, not more.

The Perverse Incentives of Managed Care

Because doctors in managed care often bear some risk for the costs of patient care, they face some of the same incentives that induce commercial health insurance companies to seek out healthy customers and avoid sick or potentially sick ones. In an article in *Health Affairs* last summer, David Blumenthal, chief of health policy research and development at Massachusetts General Hospital, explained why his recent bonuses had varied:

> Last spring I received something completely unexpected: a check for $1,200 from a local health maintenance organization (HMO) along with a letter congratulating me for spending less than predicted on their 100 or so patients under my care. I got no bonus the next quarter because several of my patients had elective arthroscopies for knee injuries. Nor did I get a bonus from another HMO, because three of their 130 patients under my care had been hospitalized over the previous six months, driving my actual expenditures above expected for this group.

Such conscious linking of specific patients to paychecks is not likely to make doctors think that their income depends on how cost-effectively they practice, as market theory would have it. Rather, they are likely to conclude, with some justification, that their income depends on the luck of the draw—how many of their patients happen to be sick in expensive ways. The payment system thus converts each sick patient, even each illness, into a financial liability for doctors, a liability that can easily change their attitude toward sick patients. Doctors may come to resent sick people and to regard them as financial drains.

Dr. Robert Berenson, who subsequently became co-medical director of an HMO, gave a moving account of this phenomenon in the *New Republic* in 1987. An elderly woman was diagnosed with inoperable cancer shortly after she enrolled in a Medicare managed care plan with him as her primary care doctor, and her bills drained his bonus account:

At a time when the doctor-patient relationship should be closest, concerned with the emotions surrounding death and dying, the HMO payment system introduced a divisive factor. I ended up resenting the seemingly unending medical needs of the patient and the continuing demands placed on me by her distraught family. To me, this Medicare beneficiary had effectively become a "charity patient."

Thus do the financial incentives under managed care spoil doctors' relationships to illness and to people who are ill. Illness becomes something for the doctor to avoid rather than something to treat, and sick patients become adversaries rather than subjects of compassion and intimacy.

THE TRUE PURPOSE OF HEALTH INSURANCE

Here is also the source of the most profound social change wrought by the American approach to cost containment. Health insurance marketing from the 1930s to the 1950s promised subscribers more reliable access to high-quality care than they could expect as charity patients. But as it is now evolving, managed care insurance will soon render all its subscribers charity patients. By tying doctors' income to the cost of each patient, managed care lays bare what was always true about health insurance: The kind of care sick people get, indeed whether they get any care at all, depends on the generosity of others.

Insurance, after all, is organized generosity. It always redistributes from those who don't get sick to those who do. Classic indemnity insurance, by pooling risk anonymously, masking redistribution, and making the users of care relatively invisible to the nonusers, created the illusion that care was free and that no one had to be generous for the sick to be treated. It was a system designed to induce generosity on the part of doctors and fellow citizens. But managed care insurance, to the extent it exposes and highlights the costs to others of sick people's care, is calculated to dampen generosity.

SELLING THE DOCTOR-AS-BUSINESSMAN

The insulation of medical judgment from financial concerns was always partly a fiction. The ideal of the doctor as free of commercial influence was elaborated by a medical profession that sought to expand its market and maintain its political power and autonomy. Now, the opposite ideal—the doctor as ethical businessman whose financial incentives and professional calling mesh perfectly—is promoted in the service of a different drive to expand power and markets. . . .

The once negative image of doctor-as-businessman has been recast to appeal to patients, as insurers, employers, and Medicare and Medicaid programs try to persuade patients to give up their old-style insurance and move into managed care plans. Doctors, the public has been told by all the crisis stories of the past two decades, have been commercially motivated all along. They exploited the fee-for-service system and generous health insurance policies to foist unnecessary and excessive "Cadillac" services onto patients, all to line their own pockets. Patients, the story continues, have been paying much more than necessary to obtain adequate, good-quality medical care. But now, under the good auspices of insurers, doctors' incentives will be perfectly aligned with the imperatives of scientifically proven medical care, doctors will be converted from bad businessmen to good, and patients will get more value for their money.

If patients knew how much clinical authority was actually stripped from their doctors in managed care plans, they might be more reluctant to join. The marketing materials of managed care plans typically exaggerate doctors' autonomy. They tell potential subscribers that their primary care doctor has the power to authorize any needed services, such as referral to specialists, hospitalization, x-rays, lab tests, and physical therapy. Doctors in these marketing materials "coordinate" all care, "permit" patients to see specialists, and "decide" what care is medically necessary. Meanwhile, the actual contracts often give HMOs the power to authorize medically necessary services, and more importantly, to define what services fall under the requirements for HMO approval.

In managed care brochures, doctors not only retain their full professional autonomy, but under the tutelage of management experts, they work magic with economic resources. Through efficient management, they actually increase the value of the medical care dollar. "Because of our expertise in managing health care," a letter to Medicare beneficiaries from the Oxford Medicare Advantage plan promised, "Oxford is able to give you 100% of your Medicare benefits and much, much more" [emphasis in original]. Not a word in these sales materials about the incentives for doctors to deny expensive procedures and referrals, nor in some cases, the "gag clauses" that prevent doctors from telling patients about treatments a plan won't cover. . . .

MEDICINE AS A HIGHER CALLING

The old cultural ideal of pure clinical judgment without regard to costs or profits always vibrated with unresolved tensions. It obscured the reality that doctoring was a business as well as a profession and that medical care costs money and consumes resources. But now that commercial managed care has turned doctors into entrepreneurs who maximize profits by minimizing care, the aspirations of the old ideal are worth reconsidering.

In trying to curb costs, we should not economize in ways that subvert the essence of medical care or the moral foundations of community. There is something worthwhile about the ideal of medicine as a higher calling with a healing mission, dedicated to patients' welfare above doctors' incomes and committed to serving people on the basis of their needs, not their status. If we want compassionate medical care, we have to structure both medical care and health insurance to inspire compassion. We must find a way, as other countries have, to insure everybody on relatively equal terms, and thus divorce clinical decisions from the patient's pocketbook and the doctor's personal profit. This will require systems that control expenditures, as other countries do, without making doctor and patient financial adversaries. There is no perfect way to reconcile cost containment with clinical autonomy, but surely, converting the doctor into an entrepreneur is the most perverse strategy yet attempted.

| "Most physicians and patients are adjusting remarkably well to the managed care revolution and . . . the quality of care remains high."

MANAGED CARE HAS NOT HARMED THE HEALTH CARE SYSTEM

David Jacobsen

In the following viewpoint, David Jacobsen maintains that managed care has not reduced the quality of health care Americans receive. He contends that the pressure doctors face under managed care is to provide optimal health care in the most efficient manner—not to deny care or provide care that is less than optimal. Jacobsen describes several procedural changes his HMO has made which he contends have lowered costs without sacrificing quality. He says that most Americans are satisfied with their health care and cites studies indicating that the quality of managed care may be higher than that under fee-for-service medicine. Jacobsen is a surgeon with Harvard Pilgrim Health Care in Boston.

As you read, consider the following questions:

1. Which does the author say is more important to patients: quality of care or greater choice of physicians?
2. What innovation has the author's HMO added to the way that its doctors perform diagnostic tests and X-rays?
3. What percentage of people were satisfied with their health care in the survey conducted by CareData Reports, as cited by Jacobsen?

"Torture by HMO" is the title of a March 18, 1996, column by Bob Herbert in the *New York Times*. Herbert tells the story of a North Carolina family with a baby suffering from leukemia. Their health maintenance organization insisted that the child undergo treatment in another state, at great cost and inconvenience. Herbert condemns the HMO's "inflexible and thoroughly inhumane" policies, adding that "humanitarian concerns are not what corporate care is about. In the competition with profits, patients must always lose."

This portrait of HMOs as soulless money-making machines has become increasingly popular in recent years, as skyrocketing health care costs have driven a shift from fee-for-service medicine to managed care. Critics such as Harvard Medical School professor David Himmelstein contend that HMOs reward doctors for providing less care, trapping them in a conflict between their incomes and their patients' welfare, and impose "gag clauses" that forbid them to discuss this conflict with patients. "The bottom line is superseding the Hippocratic oath," write Jeff Cohen and Norman Solomon in their syndicated column. "Cost-cutting edicts from HMO managements put doctors in a box. . . . Faced with directives to help maximize profits, many physicians are under constant pressure to shift their allegiance from patients to company stockholders."

CUTTING COSTS WITHOUT CUTTING QUALITY

From my perspective as both a physician and a patient in the same HMO, these charges do not ring true. I do not doubt that HMOs, like any other business, sometimes serve their customers poorly. But there is no reason to believe that managed care systematically undermines patient welfare because of the imperative to cut costs. To the contrary, I have found that efficiency is perfectly compatible with compassionate, effective health care. (Since this article was written, I have myself become a cancer patient. Thus far, my care has been unsurpassed. I have the option of being treated outside my HMO, but would not think of going anywhere else. I expect from my plan the same level of care as a patient that I have provided as a physician.)

My plan delivers care at several neighborhood health centers. Each member chooses a "home" center and a primary care physician at that center. Surgical, pediatric, obstetrical, and mental health services, as well as radiology, laboratory, pharmacy, and physical therapy, are all provided under one roof. While our "staff model" HMO does not offer as extensive a choice of physicians as many "network" HMOs, our arrangement does offer economies of scale and strict control of physician quality. Surveys consistently show that patients rate quality of care above greater choice of providers.

I am paid a straight salary and modest bonuses tied to both the plan's profitability and a patient satisfaction index. Frequent advisory audits help me and my patients sort out health care they need from health care they want. My goal is healthy, satisfied patients and a financially sound business. Every day, I put my professional reputation on the line. So does my HMO. Our challenge is to cut costs without cutting quality. Fortunately, there are many ways to do this.

OUTPATIENT CARE IS QUICKER, CHEAPER, AND OFTEN SAFER

Changing the venue of medical care from hospital to outpatient center, office, or home is the most important factor driving health care costs down and quality up. Hospitals are very expensive pieces of architecture. They are also complex places and therefore potentially hazardous to your health. Despite rigorous safeguards, medication and treatment errors can and do occur. As many as 15 percent of hospitalized patients go home with a hospital-acquired infection, often caused by antibiotic-resistant organisms. Furthermore, most patients do not wish to be in a hospital. In the last three years, my HMO has reduced hospital use by 25 percent.

Inguinal hernia repair is one of the most frequently performed operations. Just a few years ago, the cost of this operation included a preoperative night in the hospital, one to two hours in the operating room under general anesthesia, and up to five postoperative days in the hospital. The patient had to take four to six weeks off work, and the recurrence rate was 10 percent. In 1996, at my HMO, this operation requires 40 minutes of surgery in a free-standing, outpatient surgical center under local anesthesia using a $100 plastic-mesh plug. Patients have less discomfort, return to unrestricted work in one week, and enjoy a recurrence rate of less than 1 per 1,000. This approach to hernia repair has been technically feasible for several years but was usually employed sporadically, at the discretion of the surgeon or the patient. In the era of cost containment, it has rapidly become the standard in the profession, regardless of reimbursement mode.

Thanks to the innovation of laparoscopic surgery, 80 percent of my patients who need their gallbladder removed can undergo the operation as outpatients and return to work in a week. The original inspiration for this procedure was the development of miniature video cameras, and the early reports were dismissed as mere technical wizardry. But as it became clear that laparoscopic gallbladder removal was not only safe but much less expensive than conventional surgery, surgeons quickly adopted the procedure as the standard approach, and patients demanded it.

The challenge of providing better care at lower cost has spurred not only the development of new procedures but the

---

STICK TO THE FACTS ABOUT HEALTH CARE QUALITY

Repeated inaccuracies and misrepresentations about health plans can diminish consumer confidence in their health care—which is one vital reason that responsible policymakers should stick to the facts when debating the issues.

Time and again, the evidence does not support the claims about health plan practices, and the facts about quality of care in health plan settings are rarely considered or even offered. For example, despite definitive evidence from a Government Accounting Office report concluding that health plans do not use so-called "gag" clauses, opponents of managed care continue to proclaim the need for legislation banning "gag" clauses. . . .

Moreover, it is important to remember that the failed indemnity insurance system some proposals would return us to did not inspire confidence. For instance, the articles in a five part series that appeared in the *New York Times* during January 1976 included the following headlines: "Unfit Doctors Create Worry in Profession;" "Incompetent Surgery is Found Not Isolated;" "Thousands a Year Killed by Faulty Prescriptions;" and "Few Doctors Ever Report Colleagues' Incompetence." According to a report by Michael Millenson of the benefits consulting firm William M. Mercer and commissioned by the American Association of Health Plans, "[t]he abuses of fee-for-service doctors and hospitals led directly to what one could call the 'fee-for-service' backlash. It is a phenomenon that defenders of the old system seem to have forgotten."

The often proclaimed "crisis of confidence" does not affect consumers' satisfaction with their health plans. A 1997 study of about 167,000 households showed that individuals enrolled in HMOs, PPOs, and FFS report similar satisfaction levels regardless of their health status or age. Similarly, *Consumer Reports* readers were, on average, "fairly well satisfied" to "very satisfied" with their experience in 37 HMOs. A 1996 national survey of 90,000 consumers found that HMO, POS, and PPO members in poor-to-fair health were more satisfied with their health care than those in FFS.

American Association of Health Plans, *The Managed Care Debate: Correcting the Errors and Omissions*, 1998.

---

resurrection of old ones. Pilonidal abscess, a chronic and painful anorectal condition, used to be treated with radical surgery in the hospital. Recovery was frequently prolonged and painful. I now treat this problem with a 20-minute office procedure. Patients can return to work in two days, and the recurrence rate is less than 2 percent. This procedure was first described 15 years ago but languished until managed care created the incentive to implement it on a wider scale.

Open-heart surgery is expensive. Traditionally, the payer is billed separately by the hospital, the surgeon, and the anesthesiologist. My HMO recently negotiated a contract in which we pay a flat fee per operation that is about half our previous cost. As for concerns that surgeons might offer less surgery for less money, our studies show no change in mortality or morbidity since this contract went into effect. Beyond the question of ethics, no reputable provider group would risk a lucrative contract with a large HMO by delivering less than first-class care. Based on this experience, we are exploring package pricing for other high-cost procedures, such as organ transplantations.

Childhood asthma is a distressing and sometimes frightening problem for parents and children. Our studies showed that repeated visits to the emergency room were not only unnerving for families but accounted for a substantial portion of the cost of treating asthma. Through an aggressive program of family education, we are teaching our patients how to handle most asthma attacks at home, even how to give adrenaline injections. A nurse practitioner is available by telephone 24 hours a day to advise families whether a visit to the hospital may be necessary. Emergency room visits are down 40 percent in the last two years. So far, we have noted no adverse effects on patient care, and the response from families has been almost entirely positive.

HEALTH CENTERS PROVIDE MORE ACCESSIBLE CARE

Treatment of minor lacerations used to involve a trip to the hospital emergency room and frequently entailed a long wait. On nights and weekends our health centers are now staffed with specially trained physician assistants who repair 90 percent of all minor lacerations. In the first year this program has saved more than $100,000 in hospital emergency room charges while taking care of our patients better and more quickly.

For many of our patients with chronic wounds, such as bedsores and diabetic ulcers, treatment has often involved lengthy stays in rehabilitation hospitals or prolonged, expensive home visits by nurses. Under our wound-care program, most patients with chronic wounds can be treated directly at our health centers under the supervision of a physician. In most cases, patients and their families can be trained to do the daily wound care at home. In the first year, this program saved more than $70,000 in outside utilization costs.

Patients needing hip replacement surgery are often elderly and suffering from other medical problems. We now begin physical therapy evaluation in the patient's home prior to surgery. By knowing the level of family support and the location of stairs and bathrooms, we can much better prepare the patient for recuperation and rehabilitation. The new approach has cut the average hospital stay in half, eliminated the need for intermediate rehab hospital care in many cases, and accelerated recuperation.

THE FUROR OVER "DRIVE-THRU" DELIVERIES IS UNJUSTIFIED

For the past three years, my HMO has followed a policy of early discharge after childbirth. The childbirth program includes comprehensive prenatal education, post-partum home visits, and individual screening. A 16-year-old first-time mother with no family support and no telephone at home is not sent home in 24 hours. But 70 percent of women with uncomplicated vaginal deliveries are discharged in 24 to 36 hours. And despite the brouhaha over "drive-thru" deliveries, a recent survey documents that 90 percent of our patients are satisfied with their care—the same percentage as before the early discharge policy was adopted. There is no evidence that the health of mother or infant has been compromised. Most mothers and their babies belong at home with an attentive family, rather than in a potentially dangerous hospital.

Unnecessary diagnostic tests are probably the most familiar example of American medicine's spendthrift ways. Our computers are now set up so that every time a physician orders a laboratory test or X-ray procedure, a window on the screen displays the cost. Before managed care we neither knew nor asked. Preliminary analysis shows that this minor innovation has significantly reduced the ordering of routine laboratory and X-ray tests, especially among medical residents (physicians in training).

Much criticism of HMO care focuses not on common procedures such as these but on rare, emotionally charged illnesses. The cover story in the January 22, 1996, issue of *Time*, for example, chronicles the experience of a woman with advanced breast cancer whose HMO refused to pay for bone marrow transplantation. In such desperate cases, everyone understandably feels that something ought to be done. But the truth is that bone marrow transplantation for advanced breast cancer is a dangerous and expensive treatment of no proven benefit. This kind of case must be handled on an individual basis with consummate compassion and understanding, but it should not divert our attention from the myriad ways in which good medical care can be delivered for less money.

DOCTORS ADHERE TO AN ETHICAL STANDARD OF CARE

The significance of the potential conflict between physician income and patient welfare has also been exaggerated. First of all, it is offensive to me and the overwhelming majority of my colleagues to suggest that we would pad our bank accounts by obstructing or denying necessary medical care to our patients. I hew to an ethical standard of care, and so does my HMO. I am first and foremost the advocate of my patients, but always within the constraints of appropriate care and limited resources. More care is not always better care, and wishing that medicine could be exempt from the laws of economics does not make it so.

While there are various arrangements by which physicians are compensated under managed care, the incentives are to provide neither too little care nor too much care but optimal care. Under managed care, the worst course I could follow is to provide less than optimal care. Delay in diagnosis or treatment would only invite more expensive diagnosis and treatment down the line (and probably a lawsuit as well). Denying needed care is not only bad ethics; it is bad business.

As for the highly publicized "gag clauses," which have been outlawed in Massachusetts and a number of other states, my HMO does not have one. HMOs are entitled to insist on the confidentiality of proprietary information, but my HMO and most others encourage physicians to discuss financial incentives, covered benefits, and care options with patients. Many physicians are understandably dispirited by what they view as the demise of traditional health care and by projections of a 150,000-physician glut by the year 2000. But grievances and frustrations should be discussed with management and peers. Discussing them with patients can only erode an already embattled doctor-patient relationship.

MOST PEOPLE ARE SATISFIED WITH MANAGED CARE

Despite the charges of conflict and carnage, the evidence suggests that most physicians and patients are adjusting remarkably well to the managed care revolution and that the quality of care remains high. Studies have consistently shown that HMO patients are at least as satisfied with their care as patients receiving traditional fee-for-service care. A survey by CareData Reports, a New York health care information firm, revealed that, among members of 33 HMOs nationwide, nearly 80 percent were satisfied with their care. (The lowest ratings were not for quality of care but for administration and communication.) A 1994 study of 25,000 employees conducted by Xerox showed that HMO patients were significantly more satisfied with their overall care than were fee-for-service patients. In a 1994 Federal Employee Health Benefits Program survey of 90,000 federal employees, 86 percent of HMO members said they were satisfied with their plans, compared with 82 percent in fee-for-service plans. Interestingly, a 1994 survey by Towers Perrin revealed that patient satisfaction with HMO care rose with years of membership.

The results of research using objective measures have been similar. A 1996 study by KPMG Peat Marwick found that, in cities where most health care was provided by HMOs, costs were 11 percent lower, hospital stays 6 percent shorter, and death rates 5 percent lower than in cities where most care was provided under fee-for-service arrangements. A study recently published in the *Journal of the American Medical Association* looked at costs and outcomes of treatment for several chronic illnesses. Compared with fee-for-service specialists, HMO primary care physicians used 40 percent fewer hospital days and 12 percent less drugs. At four- and seven-year follow-ups, patient outcomes were the same.

A 1995 North Carolina study looked at the cost and outcome of treatment for lower-back pain. Costs for a single episode ranged from $169 in an HMO to $545 at a fee-for-service chiropractor, while outcomes were identical. As David Nash, an HMO expert at Jefferson Medical College in Philadelphia, told the *Chicago Sun-Times* in 1995, "Overwhelmingly, the published evidence supports the notion that quality of care in the managed care arena equals, if not surpasses, the care in the private, fee-for-service sector."

HIGH-QUALITY MEDICAL CARE AT AN AFFORDABLE PRICE

The shift to managed care unquestionably imposes greater responsibility on patients. More information is becoming available to enable them to compare costs and benefits and make intelligent choices. We ought to disabuse ourselves of the notion that we can have a perfect health care system in which no one is ever misdiagnosed, mismanaged, or missed altogether. But high-quality medical care at an affordable price is not only possible under managed care; it is a reality.

| "HMOs are responding to customer feedback and the market is working."

THE FREE MARKET WILL IMPROVE THE MANAGED CARE SYSTEM

Part I: Stephen Chapman, Part II: Michael W. Lynch

In the first part of the following two-part viewpoint, Stephen Chapman, a columnist and editorial writer for the *Chicago Tribune*, argues that competition forces managed care organizations to keep costs down and still provide high quality health care. Government regulation is unnecessary, he says, because if a health plan provides inferior service, patients will complain and employers will find a better one. In the second part of this viewpoint, Michael W. Lynch contends that government regulation of the managed care industry is not only unnecessary but also harmful, because it interferes with market processes that work to improve the health care system. Lynch is the Washington editor for *Reason* magazine.

As you read, consider the following questions:

1. In Chapman's opinion, if a person is dissatisfied with their HMO, what should he or she do?
2. How does Lynch define what a point-of-service option is?
3. What data from the American Association of Health Plans does Lynch cite in support of his claim that a government-mandated point-of-service option is unnecessary?

Part I: Reprinted from Stephen Chapman, "Refusing to Be Scared of Managed Care," *Conservative Chronicle*, November 20, 1996, by permission of Stephen Chapman and Creators Syndicate. Part II: Reprinted from Michael W. Lynch, "Timing Error: Politicians Just Can't Keep Up with Health Care Markets," *Reason* magazine, July 1998. Copyright 1998 by the Reason Foundation, 3415 S. Sepulveda Blvd., Suite 400, Los Angeles, CA 90034; www.reason.com.

I

Health maintenance organizations, better known as HMOs, are easy to hate. The charges against them are familiar: They take you away from your old doctor. They don't let you see a specialist without permission. They squeeze nickels until the buffalo screams. They lust after profits. They'd make saintly old Marcus Welby turn over in his grave.

No one is better acquainted with the complaints than Californians, roughly half of whom are enrolled in these allegedly money-grubbing, penny-pinching operations. As consumer activist Harvey Rosenfeld says, "HMOs have lost their traditional commitment to healing and caring. It's criminal what is happening." In November 1997, Californians got the chance to put HMOs in their place with two ballot initiatives, Prop. 214 and Prop. 216, which would have established new regulations for the ostensible protection of patients. Surprise: The voters decided they'd rather trust the market than the government.

The outcome represents a setback for the belief that no one ever went broke underestimating the intelligence of the American public. Californians were inundated with horror stories about patients who didn't get the right treatment because some HMO was too obsessed with cutting costs—and they were offered a pair of charming, painless solutions.

Both would have outlawed certain bonuses for employees, prevented HMOs from imposing so-called "gag rules" on physicians and set minimum staffing levels for health-care facilities. Prop. 216 also would have restricted premiums and levied various taxes on providers. But the voters were not persuaded that all this interference was necessary.

THE NEED FOR FISCAL RESTRAINT

Everyone agrees that medical expenditures and insurance premiums cannot be allowed to keep rising at the rate they have in recent years. HMOs are the chief instrument we have found to put a brake on costs. But whenever they take some measure to achieve this worthy goal, howls erupt from people who liked the old way of doing things just fine—and think money is no object. Thus, we get measures like Prop. 214 and Prop. 216.

Grownups understand that cutting costs is not fun. It means depriving people of things that they used to enjoy. But most of us are accustomed to the continual obligation to forgo some expenditures in order to avoid bankruptcy. HMOs, however, are the first innovation to force such unending, uncomfortable discipline on health-care spending. Small wonder that they evoke complaints from both doctors, who in the past had unfettered autonomy; and patients, who in the past could count on getting whatever treatment they wanted without laying out much of their own money.

Critics say that HMOs encourage undertreatment since their profits are the difference between the insurance premiums they receive and the cost of the care they provide. Less care equals more profits, the theory goes. But HMOs also have an incentive to attend to preventive care. Every ailment they nip in the bud is an expense they don't have to bear later.

The old fee-for-service system, of course, was thoroughly rigged in favor of overtreatment: Doctors had every reason to order lots of tests, prescribe expensive medicines and send patients off to expensive specialists. They made more money that way, at little or no cost to the patient. Those incentives got us into our current mess by sending health-care spending through the roof. They forced the shift to managed care.

HMOS MUST PLEASE PATIENTS IN ORDER TO SURVIVE

Those who oppose this development think we will all suffer as soulless bean-counters deny us needed care or shove us out of the hospital long before we are ready. But free-market capitalism creates a powerful check on such tendencies.

People who get health-insurance coverage from their employers are free to gripe, to make demands and even to change jobs if they are unhappy with their HMOs. Employers need to keep their workers passably content. If their HMOs are generating resentment among employees, managers will find other HMOs that can do better. Competition forces managed-care providers to worry about the interests of patients as well as the bottom line.

Do HMOs make mistakes? Certainly. No system created and operated by mere human beings can achieve anything approaching perfection. Being a relatively recent innovation, managed care will have to find the best methods through an endless process of trial and error. The only way to avoid occasional error is to shun anything new, which can be the biggest error of all.

The alternative to relying on HMOs is forfeiting an ever-growing share of our income to pay for medical care while getting less and less for each extra dollar we spend. Critics of managed care are engaged in a transparent fraud, assuring us we can eat all the candy we want and never gain a pound. It's a sign of progress that Californians rejected that fantasy and made peace with reality.

II

"Without reform, spending on health care will reach 19 percent of GDP (gross domestic product) by the year 2000," the White House warned ominously in an October 1993 press release. "If we do nothing, almost one in every five dollars spent by Americans will go to health care by the end of the decade, robbing workers of wages, straining state budgets and adding tens of billions of dollars to the national debt."

AMERICANS SAID "NO" TO CLINTONCARE

Well, we did nothing, at least nothing resembling the proposed ClintonCare system that promised to push every American into a government-managed health alliance. The decade is nearly ended, and American workers are again getting raises, state budgets are in the black and the central question facing Washington's budget writers is what to do with the purported surplus.

So what went right? Americans said "No" to ClintonCare and left the medical marketplace relatively free to evolve. In fact, by the time Hillary Clinton's task force got around to unveiling its notoriously bureaucratic solution, the central problem it aimed to solve—double-digit health inflation—was already a thing of the past. In 1993, total health spending increased 8.6 percent. By 1994, the private sector health market was deflating, with insurance premiums dropping 1.1 percent, according to the well-respected Mercer/Foster Higgins National Survey of Employer Sponsored Health Plans. Total health care spending as a share of GDP has held constant at 13.6 percent since 1993.

America's move to managed care put the lid on health costs. But there was a trade-off: Patients, doctors, and nurses, long accustomed to blank-check insurance, suddenly found themselves dealing with firms that limited choice. Patients found their choice of doctors restricted; doctors found their choice of medical procedures questioned by the companies paying for those procedures. This situation led to today's health care problem: the "crisis" in managed care.

HEAVY-HANDED PROPOSALS

Just as Washington wanted to solve the cost crisis in 1993 and 1994, it now wants to deploy its regulatory wisdom to remake managed care. Sen. Thomas Daschle (D-S.D.) and Rep. John Dingell (D-Mich.) are sponsoring the Patient Bill of Rights to implement the recommendations of the President's Advisory Commission on Health Care. On the other side of the aisle, Sen. Alfonse

D'Amato (R-N.Y.) and Rep. Charles Norwood (R-Ga.) are sponsoring the Patients Access to Responsible Care Act (PARCA).

These bills differ in degree, but not in their heavy-handedness. And, just as the Clintons' bureaucratizing solution to health care inflation arrived as the problem was being resolved, the current crop of health care reformers are tackling issues that health care companies, in their need to keep customers happy, are already addressing.

Mike Thompson. Reprinted by permission of Copley News Service.

Central to both the Democratic and Republican bills is a mandate on health insurers to provide a point-of-service option, which is health care jargon for being allowed to use a doctor who is not a member of the patient's insurance company's network. According to D'Amato, among the rights our federal government should secure is the "right to choose [our] own doctor."

But Americans already enjoy this right. What D'Amato really means is that government must dictate the contracts which private companies make with their customers. In this case, that means using the full force of the federal government to secure a patient's "option to see doctors outside their HMO for an additional fee."

THE MARKET IS WORKING

This provision addresses Americans' main gripe with managed care: the restrictions HMOs place on choice. But that preference is already being addressed by firms in the marketplace; after all, those companies can only prosper if they offer their customers what they want.

The American Association of Health Plans, which represents more than 1,000 managed-care companies, reports that just under 92 percent of Americans with employment-based health insurance have the choice of at least one plan that allows patients to use doctors who are not part of a company's network. Mercer/Foster Higgins data also show that the trend in health care is clearly to more open networks. From 1992 to 1997, seven in 10 Americans who left traditional indemnity plans went to preferred provider plans or point-of-service plans, which are less restrictive than traditional HMOs.

And lest they lose out competitively, HMOs now let customers go out of network. This trend started in 1996, reports *California Medicine*, when Blue Shield offered its Access+ HMO plan. To stay competitive, other firms, including Kaiser Permanente—the quintessential staff-model HMO—now offer POS options.

Even one of Washington's top HMO-bashers noted the trend, although he did so in support of his bill that would saddle HMOs with more regulations. "The health plans themselves are running ads touting the fact that they are different from the bad HMOs that don't allow their subscribers their choice of doctors, or who interfere with their doctors practicing good medicine," Rep. Greg Ganske (R-Iowa) stated on March 31.

For most people, this would be a sign that HMOs are responding to customer feedback and the market is working. But for Ganske, "This goes to prove that even HMOs know that there are more than a few rotten apples in the barrel." His assumption, of course, is that it is up to Washington's policy makers, not consumers, to sort the fruit.

LAWMAKERS DO NOT UNDERSTAND THE MARKET

Washington's best and brightest have a consistent blind spot when it comes to market processes. In October 1993, Laura D'Andrea Tyson, who then chaired the Council of Economic Advisors, claimed "market failures" were driving what was still thought to be America's health care inflation. "There is a lack of price competition in the market for insurance," Tyson wrote in a document released by the White House, "because many individuals do not have a choice of health plans."

Today's would-be reformers charge just the opposite: that individuals are deprived of a choice because intense price competition relegates them to restrictive HMOs. These criticisms are not only at odds with each other, they are at odds with reality, too.

At the very time Tyson was developing her inaccurate explanation for health care costs, intense price competition was bringing health costs down. Employers simply wouldn't continue to suffer double-digit increases in health costs, nor would their employees, who preferred such things as salary increases to gold-plated health insurance.

Similarly, as upwards of 80 percent of Americans find themselves in some sort of managed care, that industry is developing products to meet a diversity of needs. Just because Americans don't purchase their own health insurance directly doesn't mean there's "market failure." And just because employers are cost-conscious doesn't mean they have an incentive to cut corners on their health plan. They must ultimately keep their employees happy.

THE FATAL CONCEIT

Washington's lawmaking process is cumbersome. By the time laws and regulations are shaped, the information to which they are meant to respond has become outdated. But if government can't keep up with rapidly evolving markets that are experimenting with new ways to deliver products, that doesn't mean policy makers should make the work of markets more difficult.

The health care debate is a striking example of what economist and scholar Friedrich A. Hayek called the "fatal conceit": that statist ideas of rational planning can improve on the collective knowledge of thousands, as expressed through the marketplace. Perhaps health-obsessed lawmakers should study the Hippocratic Oath, which has long enjoined doctors to, "First, do no harm."

| "While HMOs are indeed 'businesses' that 'make a profit,' they are not free-market institutions, in any serious meaning of the term."

THE MANAGED CARE SYSTEM IS NOT A FREE MARKET

M. Stanton Evans

M. Stanton Evans, publisher of *Consumers' Research Magazine*, argues in the following viewpoint that the fundamental problem with the managed care system is that people do not pay for their own health care. Instead, a third party—an insurer, employer, or the government—pays. This system, he says, is antithetical to the functioning of free markets, in which consumers' purchasing decisions serve as their means of effecting change. Although managed care organizations are businesses, he says, because they have little incentive to respond to patients' concerns they are better viewed as the government's tools for rationing health care than as free market institutions.

As you read, consider the following questions:

1. What analogy does the author use to illustrate his criticism of third-party payment systems?
2. According to Evans, what determines, as he puts it, the "locus of authority" in the health care system?
3. How does Evans define "rent-seeking"?

Excerpted from M. Stanton Evans, "If You're in an HMO, Here's Why," *Consumers' Research Magazine*, December 1997. Reprinted with permission.

"Managed care" and HMOs have been the subject of countless negative stories in the press, and numerous charges that they endanger the health—and lives—of their enrollees. No day passes, it would seem, without some new allegation of care denial, people forced out of hospitals prematurely, "gag rules" for physicians, financial scandal, and a good deal else. All these matters have been the subject of congressional hearings, state and federal regulation, and action by attorneys general.

It would thus appear that "managed care," brought forward as a remedy for rising costs, is a serious problem in its own right. Arguably, it is much the greater problem if it in fact endangers lives—since rising costs, bad as they are, endanger only budgets. However, there seems to be no comprehension of why this strange scenario should be occurring: Why so many people are in "managed care," why the horror stories keep appearing, or where this knot of troubles comes from.

THIRD-PARTY PAYMENT IS THE PROBLEM

As it happens, the underlying causes for this skein of woe are fairly plain—visible to anyone who knows some basic economics, leavened with a bit of history. At the base of the health-care cost explosion—and the aftershock of "managed care"—is a bland refusal by our policy-makers to grasp and weigh the role of prices. In the usual case, indeed, the problem goes beyond this, to saying that price should be irrelevant to health care. Everyone, we hear it said, should have access to medical services as needed, regardless of ability to pay. A noble sentiment, no doubt, but as a policy fraught with peril.

In obedience to this concept, we have created a system in which the prevailing method of finance is "third-party payment"—meaning that someone other than the patient picks up the tab for service. Thanks to official policies of several kinds, some 90% of hospital costs—and more than three-quarters of all doctor bills—are now handled on this basis. The merits of this approach may be defended on welfare or other grounds, and often have been—a debatable topic which space forbids discussing; suffice it here to note that, with this system locked in place, there should be no doubt at all as to why we are facing runaway expenses. . . .

To spot the fallacy in this scheme doesn't require a course in economics; a little common sense will do just fine. Suppose you were to give 10 of your friends a duplicate of your credit card and send them to the malls to do some shopping. Since they would do the buying and you the paying, they would have no incentive to conserve on what they bought, and you would be headed for the poorhouse. Such an arrangement is so obviously dumb that nobody would dream of doing anything remotely like it. Yet this is precisely the way we pay for health care—the major difference being that it involves not 10 people, but scores of millions. . . .

MANAGED CARE EXACERBATES THE PROBLEM

It is against this backdrop of rising costs and failed controls that "managed care" has now come surging to the forefront. In one view, this is but the latest version of price controls and rationing, and it is all of that—perhaps the most iron-clad and comprehensive system of controls this country has yet seen in peacetime. It is, however, some other things as well. The rise of the HMO regime signals the morphing of our health-care system into something radically new and different—something that is the opposite of true reform, and that for prospective patients should be extremely scary.

The first thing to be observed in this respect is that HMOs not only fail to address the underlying causes of the problem, but actually serve to make them worse. That is, they promise even more third-party payment, covering still more everyday expenses, thus further boosting the upward pressure of demand. Here, for instance, is the language of one brochure from a major HMO, aimed at Medicare recipients: "No Medicare deductibles. Affordable co-payments. Unlimited hospital stays when medically necessary. Emergency care anywhere in the world. Virtually no claim forms to file. . . . Routine physical exams (preventive health services). Prescription drug discounts. Dental coverage. Vision coverage.". . .

Note in the language quoted that most of the free or nearly free things recipients are promised are routine and fairly inexpensive. This both sounds good as a recruiting pitch and may even be a source of satisfaction, for a while, once people are in the system. Patients receiving all these free or extremely low-cost things on a regular basis will probably think the set-up is a good one. And since this is all the vast majority of people need at any given time, they will show up in the surveys as customers happy with their HMO (surveys much touted by the "managed care" promoters).

What isn't addressed in all of this, however, is what happens if you get really sick, and/or require expensive treatment. Here the answers provided by HMOs are, all of a sudden, extremely fuzzy. Again refer to the language quoted—the part about "unlimited hospital stays." This sounds quite generous also, but then adds the seemingly innocuous phrase, "when medically necessary." But what, exactly, is "medically necessary"? And, equally important, who decides this? . . .

In short, while promising a vast array of benefits for everyday procedures, the HMO regime sets out to limit the big-ticket items—which in other walks of life, it may be recalled, are precisely what we want insurance policies to cover. Health coverage "managed" in this way thus completes the reversal of the insurance function: It pays routine expenses you could meet out of pocket, but tends to fade away at crunch time, when you may most desperately require it. An appropriate motto for this system would appear to be: "We're there until you need us."

THE AMERICAN WAY OF RATIONING HEALTH CARE

The main technique by which the HMOs cut back on costly treatment is something called "resource constraint," or sometimes "global budgets." What this means is that a certain fixed amount of money is assigned to health care and people who provide the service must come in within this limit. Methods of this sort are commonly used in other countries, such as Canada and England. It's often observed that these systems spend less of GDP on health care than we do, despite the fact that they have even more third-party payment. Less frequently noted is the manner in which they do this, and the results that follow. As the upward pressure of demand collides with "global budgets," care denial (particularly to older patients), technology cutbacks, and waiting lists are standard measures.

HMOs are, in essence, the American version of this concept. They undertake to provide for people's medical needs for a fixed amount of money, then "manage" the care that we receive to stay within the limits. This has effects that policy-makers—to put it as charitably as possible—don't seem to have thought through very clearly. The most obvious is to reverse completely the incentives of the cost-plus system, in which the provider gets paid more for doing more—or more elaborate—procedures. When HMOs get a fixed amount per patient, regardless of the care provided, the incentive is to deliver as little care as possible. In simplest terms, the HMO can make more money by doing less. . . .

THE QUESTION OF WHO IS PAYING

There is much more that might be said about this subject, but the foregoing should be enough to explain where all the horror stories come from. In its basic structure, albeit with several variations, the HMO is a machine for denying health care seen as being too expensive, up to and including cases in which your doctor thinks such care is needed. Note well the important point that, while all this is going on, you the patient are all but helpless. Your doctor, if you are lucky, may fight it out with the HMO in attempting to obtain some treatment for you, but you have virtually nothing to say about it. After all, he works for them, and not for you—because you are not paying.

HEALTH CARE IS NOT FAST FOOD

The patient is not a sovereign consumer informed well enough to determine whether his or her treatment is always quality care. "Medical care is fundamentally different from any other service bought or sold in our market economy," says Arnold Relman, former editor of the *New England Journal of Medicine*. "Sick people are not like consumers in a shopping mall."

Health care is not fast food. A McDonald's customer knows the taste of a hamburger, but sick people do not know what ails them, which doctor to seek out, what tests are required for diagnosis, or how their condition should be treated. Patients have to rely on physicians to determine their medical needs and to provide the required services. Market theorists disregard the fact that unlike consumers who buy ordinary products, patients rarely pay for all their medical services; they are often insured because the flat cost of services is beyond their means. Since a majority are provided health insurance by their employers, they cannot readily shift out of an HMO when they receive poor care. In any case, exercising consumer choice by switching to another plan is growing more difficult with the ongoing mergers and monopolization of HMOs.

Bernard Lown, *Hippocrates*, May 1998.

It is this factor, also, that explains why so many people have wound up, willy-nilly, in "managed care." Employers alarmed by rising premiums are looking at the bottom line, and thus quite susceptible to the cost-controlling pledges made by HMOs. Likewise, federal lawmakers and state officials, aghast at the continuing growth of health care budgets, are ready to heed the promise of tighter limits on expenses. Since these third parties are paying the bulk of the bills, they have both the incentive and the means to herd people into "managed care," with little regard for what this means in terms of treatment. Again, the question of who is paying determines the locus of authority in the system.

Politically speaking, there is one other aspect of "managed

care" that needs discussing, as it affects our prospects for doing anything about it. This is the curious manner in which the subject has been debated lately in the Congress. Over the past few years, the two political parties have basically merged positions on the issue, while not explicitly admitting they have done so. The net effect of this has been to take the question off the table—to make "managed care" a matter of bi-partisan consensus, though with collateral squabbles as to how much it should or shouldn't be subjected to regulation, and other marginalia.

HMOs and "managed care," it will be remembered, were prominent features of the Clinton health plan of 1993–94, considered essential to a "universal" system. Since such an approach would have created third-party payment to the nth degree, "managed care" was viewed as a needed measure to keep potential costs in line. This was one of the things conservative and Republican opponents of the plan denounced in urging its rejection. However, once the Republicans won the elections of 1994 and began devising health programs of their own, they immediately opted for "managed care" as well. HMOs and other types of "managed care" were central to the Republicans' Medicare-Medicaid reforms of '95 (and to those of '97 also). The GOP thus endorsed the very approach that it had so vehemently criticized under Clinton.

The causes of this strange reversal, already touched on, are fairly plain, but still the source of much confusion. Pledged to getting the federal budget under control, Republicans couldn't hope to do so without restraining Medicare and Medicaid, but for the most part had not the vaguest notion of how to do this. Enter the advocates of "managed care," saying they could do it—just sign here. Accordingly, a grateful GOP proceeded to let the friends of "managed care" draft much of its legislation. Thus did a major feature of the Clinton health plan become, with no debate whatever, a centerpiece of the "Republican Revolution."

RATIONING DEVICES, NOT FREE MARKETS

As significant as the practical effects of this reversal are the reasons put forward to explain it. According to a new breed of Republican and conservative "managed care" promoters, HMOs are simply cases of good old free enterprise in action—hence proper objects of Republican backing. HMOs, after all, are "businesses" that "make a profit," and what's wrong with that? It's now argued in these circles that HMOs should be allowed to do their thing, with minimal interference and regulation.

This is, however, a delusion, and one that—given the current vogue of markets and the GOP control of Congress—provides the HMOs with most convenient cover. In point of fact, while HMOs are indeed "businesses" that "make a profit," they are not free-market institutions, in any serious meaning of the term. In all of their main features, they are essentially the reverse—as a little reflection on their modus operandi will suggest. (For instance, in what other business that you can think of do people make more money by providing you less of what you want?)

The key to understanding HMOs and "managed care"—and the reason they work the way they do—is that they have arisen, precisely, in the absence of a market. A market exists when people pay for what they get, and make choices in response to prices. But these are, as we have seen, exactly the features that have been banished from our health-care system through third-party payment programs. It is because these crucial ingredients are missing that we have all the runaway expenses, and that HMOs are now called on to stem them. HMOs are thus a substitute for, not an extension of, free markets.

HMOS ARE GOVERNMENT SUBSIDY PROGRAMS

Beyond this, it may be said that HMOs and "managed care" as currently practiced are not merely private entities but surrogates for the state, in two related senses. First, if we view the situation as a whole, we observe a badly bloated system shaped in countless ways by acts of official policy: Subsidy programs, the tilting of the tax code, state mandates, community rating, coverage of pre-existing conditions—all counter to the normal working of free markets. The present set-up in which demand is to be controlled by fiat instead of price is the result of these repeated interventions. Rationing generally occurs when governments negate the role prices, and in this case the HMOs are the chosen rationing devices.

Second, if we focus specifically on Medicare and Medicaid, it should be apparent that what is occurring with these two programs has no resemblance to, or remote connection with, free markets. These are government subsidy programs, pure and simple, and the HMOs now busily signing up their patients are acting as vendors to, and agents of, the state. This has nothing to do with market pricing or free enterprise in general—yet it is precisely here that many Republicans in the Congress and the states, driven by the budgetary pressures, have been striving to put more people into HMOs. In these two cases, beyond all others, HMOs are simply government-authorized machines for rationing care in a non-market setting.

Finally, that HMOs are "businesses" which "make a profit"—the point on which GOP supporters and some critics of "managed care" seem most to dwell—is nothing to the purpose. There are plenty of businessmen, after all, who have raked in money from government programs of all types, from farm subsidies and housing projects to the manipulation of S&Ls. Such conduct has been all too common in our system, and even more so in other times and places where government favor has been the key to wealth and privilege. In economic jargon, such behavior is called "rent-seeking"—which is not only different from free-market conduct, but its direct antithesis.

"Rent-seeking" means the exploitation of conditions created by the state to extract returns that wouldn't exist in market situations. Such has been the common road to riches in the failed collectivisms of Eastern Europe and kleptocracies of all types around the globe. Such also was "tax farming" in the old regime of Europe, in which appointed agents of the king made their profit by mulcting the public to the limit. Plenty of money was made from such arrangements, but in no sense were they the result of markets.

The point of these reflections is more than a theoretical discussion about economics. In the current political climate, the plea that HMOs are merely free enterprise in action is being adroitly used to promote them in a Republican Congress, permit their "rent-seeking" to flourish unabated, and shield them from corrective measures by state and federal governments. Pending reform of the third-party payment system, the alibi of free markets cannot be legitimately invoked to fend off consumer safeguards against HMO abuses.

It should be stressed, however, that these considerations by themselves cannot address the fundamental problems of the HMO regime. The evil is in the very nature of the set-up. In an all-too-familiar sequence, where the basic premises of a system are mistaken, piecemeal reforms and ad hoc measures can at best redress a problem here and there, and at worst become new problems in their own right: Third-party payment leading to runaway demand; attempts to control this through price controls and rationing, and now through HMOs; then regulations laid on top of this to fend off care denial, and so on. The end result of this approach must be a layer cake of controls and regulations that in their cumulative power of interference may bring the system down entirely. The ultimate answer to this chain of woe must be, not a patchwork of further interventions, but deep-going reform of health-care finance in general.

PERIODICAL BIBLIOGRAPHY

The following articles have been selected to supplement the diverse views presented in this chapter. Addresses are provided for periodicals not indexed in the *Readers' Guide to Periodical Literature*, the *Alternative Press Index*, the *Social Sciences Index*, or the *Index to Legal Periodicals and Books*.

Bruce A. Barron	"The Price of Managed Care," *Commentary*, May 1, 1997.
Issues and Controversies On File	"Managed Health Care," May 2, 1997. Available from Facts On File News Services, 11 Penn Plaza, New York, NY 10001-2006.
Robert Kuttner	"Must Good HMOs Go Bad?" *New England Journal of Medicine*, May 21, 1998. Available from 10 Shattuck St., Boston, MA 02115-6094 or http://www.nejm.org.
Everett Carl Ladd	"Health Care Hysteria," *New York Times*, July 23, 1998.
Susan Love	"H.M.O.'s Could Save Your Life," *New York Times*, June 7, 1998.
Bernard Lown	"Physicians Need to Fight the Business Model of Medicine," *Hippocrates*, May 1998. Available from Time Publishing Ventures, Inc., 2 Embarcadero Center, Suite 600, San Francisco, CA 94111 or http://www.defendhealthcare.org.
Kathy Meis and Brant S. Mittler	"HMOs: From Cure-All to Curse," *Forbes Media Critic*, Fall 1996. Available from PO Box 3010, Harlan, IA 51593.
Linda Peeno	"Approved or Denied: How HMOs Decide What Care You Need," *U.S. News & World Report*, March 9, 1998.
Edmund D. Pellegrino	"Managed Care: An Ethical Reflection," *Christian Century*, August 12–19, 1998.
Time	"Playing the HMO Game," cover story, July 13, 1998.
Peter Wehrwein	"Why Managed Care Gets a Bad Rap," *Managed Care Magazine*, February 1997. Available from Stezzi Communications, 301 Oxford Valley Rd., Suite 1105A, Yardley, PA 19067 or http://www.managedcaremag.com.

CHAPTER 3

WHAT GOVERNMENT INITIATIVES COULD IMPROVE THE HEALTH CARE SYSTEM?

Chapter Preface

On January 14, 1998, President Bill Clinton joined other leading Democrats in announcing their plan for a "Patients' Bill of Rights"—a new law that would guarantee certain benefits to patients enrolled in managed care plans. "By passing a Patients' Bill of Rights—setting national standards—we can make sure that all Americans have the same right to health care, no matter what plan their employer chooses, how that plan is funded, or what state they live in," said Senator Tom Daschle of South Dakota. Republicans responded with their own patient protection bills. Representative Charlie Norwood of Georgia described the Republicans' Patient Access to Responsible Care Act (PARCA) as "a single, simplified set of federal patient protections, modeled closely after the standards already in use by most of the states and the Medicare system."

Both of these patient protection laws would have allowed patients to see doctors outside their health plan's network of physicians, and required health plans to cover necessary emergency-room care. Both would have established procedures for patients to appeal the denial of health services or payment by seeking review from an independent panel of medical experts. The major difference between the bills concerned the ability of patients who feel they have been wronged to sue their health plans. The Democratic bill would have made it easier for patients to sue HMOs and employer-sponsored health plans, while the Republican proposal would have limited the amount that patients could obtain for the denial of health benefits.

No patient protection bill was passed into law in 1998. However, candidates from both parties made HMO reform a major part of their platforms in the 1998 congressional elections. Shortly after the elections, Clinton and Daschle both vowed to revive the Patients' Bill of Rights in the 106th Congress.

Many observers believe that these patient protection laws are part of the government's overall strategy to improve the health care system through a series of incremental reforms. President Clinton's failure to enact comprehensive health care reform in 1994, write Judith Feder and Larry Levitt of the Department of Health and Human Services, "indicates that health care reform can be achieved only in steps." The authors in the following chapter debate some of the ways in which the government might improve the health care system without dramatically disrupting its current framework.

| "The Patients Protection Act would help restore Americans' confidence that providing quality health care is the first priority of all insurers."

PATIENT PROTECTION LAWS WOULD IMPROVE THE HEALTH CARE SYSTEM

Barbara Boxer

In the following viewpoint, Barbara Boxer maintains that laws are needed to protect patients from abusive managed care practices. Boxer advocates a law that would set a new standard for the type of emergency room care that health insurance plans are required to cover, require health plans to refer patients to specialists outside the plan's network when necessary, and remove a federal restriction on how health plans may be sued. She contends that these regulations enjoy widespread public support and are necessary to ensure the quality of care that managed care organizations provide. Boxer is a Democratic senator from California.

As you read, consider the following questions:

1. What percent of consumers support patient protection laws, according to the author?
2. According to Boxer, in what situations would the Patients Protection Act require insurers to cover emergency care?
3. What authority does the author say the Patients Protection Act would give to states?

In the summer of 1994, Joyce Ching began to experience abdominal pain so severe that some days she could not muster the strength to play with her 5-year-old son, Justin. Her health-maintenance organization's, or HMO's, primary-care physician recommended only that she modify her diet rather than immediately see a specialist.

As the months passed, Joyce's pain worsened and sometimes was accompanied by rectal bleeding. There were times when she couldn't even get out of bed. And still her doctor refused to refer her to a specialist; he just told her to change her diet again. Finally, after nearly three months of suffering, Joyce's doctor referred her to a qualified gastroenterologist, who quickly made the correct diagnosis—advanced colon cancer. But it was too late. Joyce died at age 34, leaving behind her husband, David, and son, Justin.

Joyce Ching didn't have to die so young. Had her HMO referred her to a gastroenterologist experienced in diagnosing colon cancer, she might be alive today.

The Patient Protection Movement

Stories like Joyce's are driving the nationwide movement for patient protections. Too many of us have a family member or a friend who has been mistreated by an HMO. Independent surveys show an astonishing 80 percent of consumers believe insurance plans often compromise the quality of care to save money. Ninety percent believe a patient protection act is needed to guarantee quality health care. This tremendous distrust of the managed-care system almost is universal: When Helen Hunt's character in the movie *As Good As It Gets* berated her HMO for denying needed respiratory care to her young son, audiences everywhere understood and cheered wildly.

No one advocates the abolition of HMOs and other managed-care plans. To their credit, HMOs have placed a new and needed emphasis on preventive care, such as childhood immunization and prenatal care. To the overall benefit of the health-care system, they also have been able to slow the explosive inflation of health-care costs. But in their zeal to cut costs, some HMOs have cut corners.

Since 1996, more than two dozen bills have been introduced in Congress to guarantee basic rights for patients enrolled in managed-care health plans. Competing proposals have been introduced by both Democrats and Republicans and are supported by groups and individuals spanning the ideological spectrum. Clearly, the concern expressed at the grassroots level has been heard in Washington.

In an extraordinary demonstration of cooperation, Democratic leaders in the House of Representatives and the Senate brought together the leading members of Congress advocating managed-care reform. We sat around a table and discussed the very best ideas of all the proposals under consideration.

The result of that collaborative process is the Patients Protection Act of 1998. House and Senate Democrats—joined by a handful of courageous Republicans and the American Medical Association—believe this bill will restore Americans' confidence that medical decisions always will come before business decisions. . . .

The Patients Protection Act [also known as the Patients' Bill of Rights] would require that all health plans meet the following requirements:

GUARANTEEING ACCESS TO CARE

Provide fair access to emergency services. As a cost-saving measure, many managed-care plans require patients to obtain preauthorization before receiving emergency care. If a patient visits an emergency room without advance permission, the insurance plan can refuse to pay if the final diagnosis uncovers only minor health problems.

Denying coverage for emergency care discourages people suffering from potentially life-threatening symptoms, such as severe chest pain, from seeking immediate treatment. Responsible health-care providers should send the opposite message to their patients: If you believe that you are experiencing a life-threatening emergency, seek help immediately—call 911, not your insurance agent!

The Patients Protection Act fixes this problem by requiring insurers to cover emergency care in situations that a prudent layperson would consider life-threatening.

Guarantee access to specialty care. Perhaps the most common complaint about managed-care plans is that they limit access to qualified specialists and require patients to meet unnecessary and time-consuming obstacles to obtain a referral. Joyce Ching's HMO, for example, refused her repeated requests for a referral to a specialist—a decision with, in her case, possibly fatal consequences.

The Patients Protection Act requires that patients be referred to a qualified specialist when medically appropriate. If an HMO does not employ a physician with the expertise to treat a serious health problem, it must provide one outside its service network at no extra charge. The bill also requires insurers to provide standing referrals for patients with chronic conditions requiring repeat specialty care.

DEALING WITH DENIALS FOR TREATMENT

Institute an independent appeals process. When health plans deny needed care, patients and their doctors deserve the right to appeal and receive a timely decision. Although most managed-care plans have some kind of grievance process, the person or committee deciding the appeal often is employed by the insurer that denied the claim in the first place. Patients cannot expect an impartial hearing from an arbitrator with such a clear conflict of interest.

The Patients Protection Act requires that appeals in life-threatening cases be heard by an outside party with medical and legal expertise. Decisions must be made within 72 hours and are binding on the health plan.

PUBLIC OPINION ON GOVERNMENT SPONSORED CONSUMER PROTECTIONS IN MANAGED CARE

Favor: "The government needs to protect consumers from being treated unfairly and not getting the care they should from HMOs and managed care plans."

Oppose: "Additional government regulation is a bad idea/it isn't worth it and would raise the cost of health insurance too much for everyone."

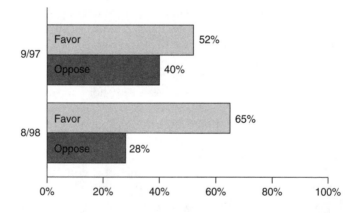

Source: Preliminary data from Kaiser/Harvard national survey of Americans (conducted 8/98); Kaiser/Harvard National Survey of Americans' Views on Managed Care, November 1997 (conducted 9/97).

Hold health plans accountable for medical decisions. Through their coverage decisions, health plans have become increasingly involved in medical decisions. In fact, some experts have argued that insurance-company executives actually are practicing medicine without a license. It is easy to understand why. If, for example, an insurer declares a cutting-edge treatment experimental and refuses to cover it, that decision has as great an impact on a patient's course of treatment as the advice of any doctor. Yet, because of a quirk in federal pension law, health plans cannot be held legally responsible for these decisions.

Under current law, if a doctor fails to recommend a potentially lifesaving test to a patient, and the patient dies as a result, the doctor can be sued for malpractice. However, if this same patient fails to take the test because his HMO refuses to cover it, and also dies as a result, the patient's family has virtually no legal recourse. It's no wonder that California's distinguished District Court Judge William G. Young wrote that the federal law, known as ERISA, "has evolved into a shield of immunity that protects health insurers, utilization-review providers and their managed-care entities."

The Patients Protection Act gives states the authority to determine whether patients should be allowed to sue health plans for negligent medical decisions. The bill does not create a new cause of action by itself; it simply allows states to decide how to treat health plans as medical and legal entities.

GIVING PATIENTS THE INFORMATION THEY NEED

Ban gag rules and improper financial incentives. Open communication is the cornerstone of a healthy doctor-patient relationship. Yet some managed-care plans interfere with doctors' discussions with their patients by limiting their ability to discuss expensive treatment options. Others have fee structures that reward doctors for failing to refer patients to specialists and penalize them for issuing too many referrals. These gag rules and improper financial incentives undermine the doctor-patient relationship and can jeopardize patients' health by discouraging needed specialty care.

Disclose needed consumer information. It is essential that consumers have the information they need to make the best possible health-care decisions. But too often, key plan information—such as the financial incentives offered to health-care providers—are difficult to obtain, if they are available at all.

To give consumers the information they need to choose a health plan, the Patients Protection Act requires insurers to provide basic information about their plan to all new enrollees. This includes an explanation of covered and excluded services, the process for filing appeals and grievances and measurements of customer satisfaction with the plan. More extensive information, including the details of financial arrangements between the insurer and health-care providers, must be made available upon request.

Provide protection for women. Women have special health-care needs that often are not addressed by managed-care providers. For example, many HMOs require women to receive a referral for routine obstetrical and gynecological care. Requiring such referrals is a waste of time for both a woman and her primary-care physician. For obstetrical and gynecological care, OB/GYNs are our primary-care providers.

The Patients Protection Act permits direct access to OB/GYNs, and allows women to designate OB/GYNs as their primary-care providers. It also prevents plans from imposing arbitrary time limits on hospital stays after mastectomies—ending the despicable practice of "drive-by" mastectomy surgery.

A Commonsense Approach to Health Care

The many provisions of the Patients Protection Act would help restore Americans' confidence that providing quality health care is the first priority of all insurers. By focusing on the most important goals—guaranteeing access to specialists and emergency care, implementing an independent appeals process, banning gag rules and requiring full disclosure—House and Senate Democrats are confident that we have produced legislation addressing our constituents' legitimate concerns, at a very low cost and with minimal government intervention.

Powerful interest groups, led by the insurance industry and their allies in Congress, have vowed to do whatever it takes to block this bill from passing—or even reaching the Senate floor. But we are just as determined to make sure it becomes law. Our secret weapon in this battle is the support of the American people—90 percent of whom believe reforms are needed to protect patients' rights. The Patients Protection Act enjoys such strong support because it offers a commonsense approach to health care and because health economists estimate the costs would be minimal—that's why many good HMOs already are implementing similar reforms.

"By trying to force managed care companies to expand the benefits they offer to their current policyholders, Republicans and Democrats are hurting the millions of Americans who cannot afford health insurance at all."

PATIENT PROTECTION LAWS WOULD NOT IMPROVE THE HEALTH CARE SYSTEM

Part I: Brian J. LeClair, Part II: Jonathan Chait

In the following two-part viewpoint, Brian J. LeClair, vice president of a health insurance brokerage agency, and Jonathan Chait, an associate editor of *New Republic*, argue that patient protection laws will not improve the health insurance system. In Part I, LeClair argues that such laws would force health insurers to raise their premiums, with the result that more people would be unable to afford health insurance. In Part II, Chait contends that patient protection laws are part of the government's strategy to improve the health care system with incremental reforms, a strategy Chait believes cannot work.

As you read, consider the following questions:

1. In LeClair's opinion, why would the patient protection laws the Democrats have proposed raise premiums higher than Republican bills would?
2. What is the main flaw of the current health insurance system, according to Jonathan Chait, and how does it let people, in his words, "game the system"?

Republicans and Democrats have been touting their separate bills to overhaul managed care, while sniping at the other party's legislation. . . .

HURTING THE UNINSURED

But both parties' bills are flawed—and for the same reason. By trying to force managed care companies to expand the benefits they offer to their current policyholders, Republicans and Democrats are hurting the millions of Americans who cannot afford health insurance at all.

That's because the specific provisions of the Democratic and Republican bills would be quite costly, virtually guaranteeing that H.M.O.'s would be forced to raise their rates, which are already high enough. Indeed, if any of the current bills were to be enacted, individuals who can now barely afford insurance may find themselves priced out of the market.

This would contribute to an already unfortunate trend. In 1993, there were 37 million Americans—most of them working class—who were without any health insurance. Since then, the uninsured population has increased by almost 20 percent. Today, more than 44 million Americans, or one in six, are without any coverage, including Medicaid or Medicare.

The rise is not surprising, given the cost of health insurance. Today, basic insurance for a family of four in Minnesota, for example, costs $346 a month, and that's only for families that qualify for the best rates. Most families would be forced to pay more—some as much as $578 per month.

COSTLY MANDATES

Yet, the Republican and Democratic bills only make this problem worse. The Democratic plan has the potential to do more damage, because it allows patients to sue their H.M.O.'s when they are dissatisfied with their coverage. The costs of litigation would most likely increase the cost of premiums, leading to even more uninsured.

The House and Senate Republican plans are better, because they don't allow lawsuits. And they support the expansion of medical savings accounts, which are now available to individuals, tax free, on a limited basis. This plan would allow people to buy lower-cost insurance with high deductibles and to pay for routine medical care through these accounts.

But the Republicans' bill, especially the Senate version, also has costly mandates. H.M.O.'s, for instance, would be required to pay for many dubious emergency room visits, turning these special units into the functional equivalent of an ordinary doctor's waiting room.

In addition, patients would be allowed to go outside an H.M.O. network to receive treatment from any willing doctor, paying only a portion of the cost. Such a requirement cuts right to the heart of managed care's ability to cut costs and make health care affordable, by obliterating the significant savings that H.M.O.'s can obtain by contracting only with doctors who agree to their payment plans.

THE REAL HEALTH CARE CRISIS

These mandates, however popular with the public, don't address our real health crisis, the increasing number of uninsured. Yet Republicans have embraced them anyway and seem interested in mitigating only the very worst parts of the Democratic bill.

Democrats and Republicans should start worrying about those really at risk—the men, women and children who have no hope of being able to ante up the estimated $5,280 a year needed to insure that they, too, can receive quality medical care.

II

Ever since President Clinton's health care reform met its untimely demise in 1994, conventional wisdom has held that the plan was a victim of its own excessive ambition. The thinking was that if only Clinton had sought from the outset to achieve universal coverage through small, incremental steps, instead of trying for universal coverage all at once in a fit of hubristic Rodhamism, the reform effort would have succeeded.

BITE-SIZED HEALTH CARE REFORMS

Since then, members of both parties, including the president, have acted upon this view, slowly putting into place a new regime of bite-sized health care reforms. In the summer of 1996, Republican Senator Nancy Kassebaum of Kansas joined with Democratic Senator Ted Kennedy of Massachusetts to propose a bill guaranteeing that people who switched or lost their jobs could buy insurance. After Clinton endorsed the Kassebaum-Kennedy bill, it eventually passed the Senate unanimously. In 1997, Kennedy teamed up with another Senate Republican, Orrin Hatch of Utah, to demand health coverage grants for uninsured children. Clinton successfully included such a measure in the bipartisan budget bill. Since then, he has proposed a "bill of rights," setting federal standards for the treatment of patients by health plans, such as the guarantee of emergency room care. And he is reportedly considering a new program to help the "near elderly"—those between the ages of 54 and 65—obtain medical coverage.

These incremental measures, both proponents and foes agree, essentially amount to the Clinton Plan chopped up into digestible nuggets. "If what I tried before won't work, maybe we can do it another way," said Clinton in a speech in 1997. "That's what we've tried to do, a step at a time, until we eventually finish this." The congressional Republican leadership is fighting these reforms for the very same reason Clinton supports them. "It is clear that these initiatives are a Trojan horse for implementing the once-defeated Clinton plan," Senate Majority Leader Trent Lott and Majority Whip Don Nickles wrote in a memo to fellow congressmen. Conservatives hope to kill the new reforms by associating them with the old reforms. HMO lobbyist Karen Ignagni told *The New York Times*: "It's beginning to feel a lot like 1993."

Reprinted by permission of Chuck Asay and Creators Syndicate.

But it's not like 1993, at least politically, in that this time it's the Republicans—not Clinton—who are getting flogged. Kassebaum-Kennedy and kiddiecare eventually sailed through virtually without public opposition, and Clinton's bill of rights is registering Mother Teresa–like approval levels in opinion polls. The few naysayers—insurance lobbies and their conservative allies in Congress—have been stymied by massive Republican defections. Some of the most stringent new HMO regulations, in fact, are sponsored by Republican Representative Charlie Norwood of Georgia and Senator Al D'Amato of New York. "Once these bills hit the floor, it's real hard to oppose them," Bill Gradison, president of the Health Insurance Association of America, conceded to *Congressional Quarterly*.

GAMING THE SYSTEM

There's a good reason for this shift. Incremental reform is not politically equivalent to sweeping health care reform because it is not substantively equivalent to it, either. Incrementalism doesn't seek to change the perverse incentives of the current market-driven system, nor does it address the issue of health care costs. This is, of course, part of the reason why it's so popular. It's also why, as a matter of policy, it will likely disappoint.

To understand this paradox, step back for a moment and consider the rationale for health care reform. The main flaws with the current system revolve around the fact that it is voluntary. Employers can choose whether or not to cover their workers; individuals can choose whether or not to buy insurance. This lets people game the system: healthy people choose to forego insurance coverage until they become sick, while insurance companies do the same thing right back by trying to exclude high-risk cases and cover only low-risk ones.

Since voluntarism is what ails the system, the heart of any systematic solution ought to be compulsion. But compulsion creates losers—it forces companies to pay for their employees' health care, or people to buy their own insurance. Incrementalism avoids this unpleasantness. It doesn't require that any employer pay for health care, and it doesn't force anyone into an insurance pool. No wonder incrementalism appeals so much to politicians.

Except that expanding coverage in this fashion isn't quite as easy as it sounds. Consider the Kassebaum-Kennedy law, which was designed to help prevent insurance companies from denying coverage to people with a high risk of getting sick, a practice known as skimming. Kassebaum-Kennedy didn't attack all skimming. Rather, it focused on a particular kind of skimming, in which people who have insurance change their jobs and are subsequently denied coverage, typically because of a preexisting health condition. The law required insurance companies to offer coverage to anybody who had previously been insured, which most people consider fair.

But the law didn't require insurance companies to offer job-switchers coverage *at the same rates* they previously paid. So while somebody with a chronic condition like diabetes won't lose coverage if he switches jobs, chances are he'll have to pay a lot more for it—quite possibly more than he can afford. Kennedy-Kassebaum could have prohibited such price discrimination, of course, but that would have created other problems. Since it costs more to insure the sick than it does to insure the healthy, the insurance companies would have had to pass on increases to everyone—which, in turn, would have caused more healthy people to drop out of the plans completely.

This trade-off is inescapable without a universal system. Insuring more sick people, which may be a good idea, means insuring fewer healthy people. Forbidding insurers to choose whether or not to offer coverage while still allowing individuals to choose whether or not to buy insurance inherently creates these kinds of perversities and instabilities.

THE CROWDING-OUT EFFECT

Another problem with incrementalism arises when the government tries to cover an uninsured population in a system in which employers can decide whether or not to insure their workers. Take, for instance, the child health care law—kiddie-care—which offered federal grants to states to cover uninsured children. The rationale is straightforward. Children in very-low-income families get insurance through Medicaid, while those in higher-income families generally receive coverage from their parents' employers. Kiddiecare aims to cover the kids in between. A state could insure kids in families that earn, say, up to two or three times the poverty level—where you're likely to find parents working in part-time and low-paying jobs that typically don't offer health insurance.

Again, that's a fine idea. But, inevitably, even at lower income levels, you'll be offering insurance to at least some families who already get it through their jobs. This will create a perverse incentive to the good employers—who now offer coverage—to stop doing so. Why should they pay, after all, if the taxpayers will pick up the tab instead?

This phenomenon is called the crowding-out effect, and it neatly illustrates the limits of incrementalism. Partial coverage can work with populations that don't have insurance on their own—the elderly and the extreme poor, for example. But the more the government steps in with other groups, the more the private sector steps back. It is impossible to design a system in which the private sector decides whom to insure and the government insures everybody else. This is why Clinton's goal—universal coverage through incremental steps—cannot happen. In order to achieve universal coverage, either all businesses must be forced to cover their employees (which is what made his 1993 plan politically unpassable), or the government must cover everybody.

REJECTING INCREMENTALISM

So what's wrong with the government covering everybody? Absolutely nothing, if—and only if—it's part of an overhaul of the entire health care system. Simply extending coverage to one group at a time—children, the near-elderly—until the state is paying for everybody isn't the same thing as a systematic overhaul. Achieving universal coverage by incrementally layering new programs would be prohibitively expensive. "The more steps you put into a system," observes Joe White, a health care specialist at the Twentieth Century Fund, "the more money sloshes away in administration and intergovernmental fights."

That kind of inefficiency might sound like nothing more than an annoying side-effect until you consider the original reasons for overhauling the health care system in the first place. Remember, the problem with our system is not just that millions go without insurance. We also have the costliest health care in the world. The point of systematic overhaul was to cover everybody *and* save money. That's why reformers in 1993 explicitly rejected incrementalism, which simply reinforces the irrationalities of the status quo.

Cost control, then, represents the most dramatic difference between health care reform four years ago and health care reform today. Clinton's 1994 plan was an effort to restrain health care spending by harnessing market forces. Incrementalism is an effort to restrain the market forces themselves. It is in this way, ironically, what Clinton is doing now is actually more liberal than what he was doing then.

And that's exactly why it's so politically successful. The public didn't turn against the Clinton plan because it imposed regulations on insurance companies or because it instituted an employer mandate. What the public feared—what Harry and Louise said they feared—was being herded into managed care. Business and insurance lobbies cultivated and preyed upon this anxiety to kill reform in 1994; now Clinton has coopted this same fear and turned it against his old enemies. Somewhere, Hillary Rodham Clinton and Ira Magaziner must be enjoying the joke.

> "Nothing . . . except ensuring that patients have the right to sue managed care plans, will prevent [managed care's] unconscionable acts of violence against patients."

PATIENTS SHOULD BE ABLE TO SUE THEIR HEALTH PLANS

Linda Peeno

In the following viewpoint, Linda Peeno argues that giving patients the right to sue managed care organizations is the only way to hold them accountable for denying necessary medical care to their patients. She describes a federal law that places limits on the types of damages that health plans are liable for and insists that this law be changed. Peeno was formerly the medical director of a managed care company, and claims that in that role she was pressured into denying treatments in order to save her company money. She now works as a managed care consultant and chairs the Hospital Ethics Committee at the University of Louisville School of Medicine in Kentucky.

As you read, consider the following questions:

1. How does Peeno describe her former job duties as medical director of a managed care company?
2. What does ERISA stand for?
3. According to Peeno, what is the only measure in patient protection legislation that can help prevent managed care abuses?

Reprinted from Linda Peeno, "Patients Are the Losers When Medical Practice Is Free of Liability," Los Angeles Times, October 9, 1998, by permission of the author.

I magine entrusting your life to a doctor who can do whatever he or she wants without concern for the consequences. Would you submit to surgery by the hands of someone who could never be sued for making a wrong cut? Most of us cringe at the idea, because we want our doctors to be accountable for what they know, what they do, the decisions they make, the effects they have on our bodies.

When I was a medical director working for a managed care company, I used to worry about the decisions I made. My job, as the company doctor, was to decide what patients could and could not have, and what their physicians could and could not do. This is what the industry calls making "medical necessity" determinations. I had the final medical word. Call it what you will, couch it in whatever language you want, it simply means that I practiced medicine on patients I never saw, touched or heard.

This troubled me. There were areas of medicine that I did not know about. Even if it was an area of my own knowledge and expertise, I rarely had enough information to make good decisions. Keeping numbers low defined the success of my job. That meant denials—surgeries, admissions to the hospital, additional days once there, X-rays, lab tests, visits to specialists. And when I denied a service or procedure that a treating physician requested, I did not have to look into the eyes of a frightened, suffering patient whose very life might depend upon the medical need I withheld with the stroke of a pen.

Who watched the medicine I practiced? No one, I discovered, not even lawyers.

Early into this work, I received a call from a physician seeking authorization for surgery for cancer in an elderly patient. At first, I approved it. However, my supervisor—another physician—reprimanded me for this, telling me that it was clear that the man was old and was nearly dead from his cancer. Surgery would do no good. I should have denied this.

A Shield Called ERISA

I made many kinds of arguments against this kind of thinking, including a concern about my liability when the man died. The other doctor's response stunned me. He said: "We don't have to worry about that. HMOs and company doctors can't be sued for malpractice. We have a shield called ERISA."

So I learned early into my work that ERISA was the magic term.

I had left my managed health care insurance jobs and was enrolled in law classes before I discovered that "ERISA" refers to the misleadingly titled Employee Retirement Income Security Act, a 1974 federal law that prevents nearly 125 million Americans from collecting damages for denial of medical treatment that results in death, injury or economic loss. ERISA allows people to recover only the benefits they were entitled to in the first place. For example, if they were denied an MRI test that would have diagnosed their cancer, and then died for lack of treatment, their families would be entitled to sue only for the cost of the MRI.

THE ABSURDITY OF ERISA

A recent case emanating from Kentucky illustrates the absurdity of the ERISA remedial system. Frank Wurzbacher had the misfortune of contracting prostate cancer. To deal with his condition, Mr. Wurzbacher received periodic injections of leupron. Under his health plan, these treatments—costing $500 per injection—were supposed to be fully covered. When Prudential took over as the plan administrator, Mr. Wurzbacher was told that he would have to pay $180 per injection—an amount he could not afford. As a result, Mr. Wurzbacher asked his physician for health care alternatives. In light of the aggressiveness of his cancer, Wurzbacher's doctor said that his only alternative was castration.

Prudential approved the castration operation and Mr. Wurzbacher was castrated. When Wurzbacher returned home from the hospital, he found a letter from Prudential notifying him that it had made a mistake and that the plan would pay the full $500 for the leupron injections.

When Mr. Wurzbacher brought suit under state law, his claim was denied due to ERISA preemption. More significantly, if Mr. Wurzbacher brought suit under the provisions of ERISA, his only available "remedy" would be the provision of leupron injections at no cost. Obviously, this "remedy" constitutes a non-remedy and is entirely useless for Mr. Wurzbacher. ERISA, in this and many other cases, constitutes a cruel and unusual joke for someone who experienced tragic harm due to the health plan administrator's negligence.

Ronald F. Pollack, statement on ERISA Preemption, given before the Senate Appropriations Committee, May 14, 1998.

Little wonder then that health plans can, with no regard for effects on patients, send a patient to a substandard facility or to an incompetent physician; deny or delay access to necessary specialists or treatments; write ill-founded medical guidelines and hire non-medical persons to apply them, and pay physicians in ways that cause him or her to deny or limit care.

These are just some of the ways money is saved at the expense of life and well-being of real people. With ERISA protection, health plans and medical directors never have to confront their patients. They never have to account for the consequences of their medical decisions. If any decisions result in harm or death, so be it. Patient lives and experiences are "just anecdotes," just the price of doing business. And to compound the indignity, they take the patients' own premium money to cover up their acts with self-promotional public relations campaigns.

HEALTH PLANS MUST BE HELD ACCOUNTABLE

In my current work as a health care consultant, I review plans and patient experiences every day. Even with my inside knowledge about how HMOs work, I continue to be surprised at what is done to unsuspecting patients by unregulated, cavalier, negligent health plans. Incompetent, cruel medical directors. Cold, calculated elimination of expensive patients. Employees with little more than high school education making complex, urgent medical decisions. You name it, I have seen it. Nothing in any patient protection bill yet proposed, except ensuring that patients have the right to sue managed care plans, will prevent these unconscionable acts of violence against patients.

Let's be honest: The heart of managed care is the practice of medicine by corporations and their company doctors. Their distance from the patient does not mute the damage done when their medical decisions are negligent, dangerous or simply ignorant. To continue to allow them to practice behind the ERISA shield is like giving our physicians the freedom to do, or not do, whatever they want, with no recourse against them for our harm or death. Surely we will not continue to be that foolish.

> "[If health plans are exposed to medical liability lawsuits,] the health care system will become more adversarial, alienating consumers, health plans, and providers."

PATIENTS SHOULD NOT BE ABLE TO SUE THEIR HEALTH PLANS

Karen Ignagni

Karen Ignagni is president of the American Association of Health Plans (AAHP), a trade association representing managed care organizations. In the following viewpoint, she maintains that increasing patients' ability to sue their health plans will reduce health care quality rather than improve it. Increasing health plans' medical liability, she says, will force managed care organizations to more closely monitor doctors' decisions and to raise insurance premiums. A better way of dealing with disputes, the author concludes, is to resolve problems before a patient sustains an injury rather than compensating victims after they have been harmed.

As you read, consider the following questions:

1. Approximately how many health plans does the AAHP represent, according to the author?
2. According to Ignagni, how would giving patients the ability to sue health plans affect the way in which medical decisions are made?
3. What measures does Ignagni believe would be a "more appropriate means for meeting consumer needs than increased exposure to litigation"?

Excerpted from Karen Ignagni, "Health Managed Care Standards and Regulation," testimony before the U.S. House Committee on Commerce, Subcommittee on Health and Environment, October 28, 1997.

I am Karen Ignagni, President and Chief Executive Officer of the American Association of Health Plans (AAHP), which is the principal national trade association representing HMOs, PPOs, and other network-based health plans throughout the United States. The Association represents approximately 1,000 member plans serving over 150 million Americans—over half of the population. AAHP and its members are dedicated to a philosophy of care that puts patients first by providing coordinated and comprehensive health care. . . .

We question whether The Patient Access to Responsible Care Act of 1997 or The Health Insurance Bill of Rights Act of 1997 represent the appropriate role of government in health care. They duplicate current state and federal regulations and oversight, and propose a degree of federal micromanagement that both threatens health plans' ability to continue to innovate and suggests a return to the failed old system. . . .

HEALTH PLANS MUST BE ABLE TO DECIDE WHAT CARE IS MEDICALLY NECESSARY

[The latter bill] would undermine health plans' ability to promote appropriate and affordable care by requiring that health plans cover any care determined to be medically necessary by the treating physician. This provision ignores the role health plans play, as part of making coverage determinations, in improving the quality of care.

The large volume of inappropriate care—much of which is harmful—that Americans have received is well documented. Therefore purchasers and plans state in their contracts that the benefits they offer will be covered benefits only when medically necessary. Over the past 20 years, health plans have been successful in addressing fundamental quality of care issues by working with physicians to reduce inappropriate care and by their involvement in reviewing medical necessity decisions for the purpose of making coverage determinations. In the mid-1970s, when fee-for-service dominated the market, the House Government Operations Subcommittee estimated that there were some 2.4 million unnecessary operations performed every year—many of them unnecessary hysterectomies and cesarean-section deliveries. Based on the medical literature, it was estimated that as many as 15,000 Americans died each year from unnecessary operations and many more were injured.

Health plans work to address this problem. For example, plans working with physicians have identified instances where heart transplants have been recommended for patients who needed less aggressive coronary bypasses instead. Similarly, they have identified instances where kidney transplants have been recommended for patients who needed more aggressive kidney-pancreas transplants. Notably, there also is considerable evidence from peer-reviewed studies that health plan members obtain access to appropriate medical care. . . .

Moreover, it is important that we not lose sight of one basic fact inherent in our health care system—health insurance is a legal contract to provide certain benefits. It is not, and never has been, a promise to pay for every medical service, whether medically necessary or not. If health plans are forced to cover certain care even in the face of substantial evidence that the treatment is inappropriate for that patient or may even cause harm, plans will lose much of their ability to work with physicians to reduce inappropriate overutilization and underutilization. . . .

OPENING THE FLOODGATES OF LITIGATION

The key to a quality health care system is continuously finding effective ways to address problems before patients are harmed rather than compensating them long after an injury or even death.

The most incongruous aspect of The Patient Access to Responsible Care Act is that, while it undermines health plans' ability to hold physicians accountable for delivering quality, affordable care, it at the same time exposes health plans and other insurers, their employees, administrators, employers voluntarily offering health benefits to employees, and anyone else involved in the business of providing or arranging for health benefits coverage to state tort liability. This provision's apparent purpose is to eliminate ERISA preemption of state law causes of action to recover damages for personal injury. Its practical effect will be to open the floodgates of litigation, leading to higher health care costs system-wide with no proven effect on the quality of health care provided to Americans. . . .

The increase in litigation will have far-reaching effects on patients, beyond the cost increases that will put coverage out of reach for many. Patients will lose as physicians and health plans are pitted against each other. As noted in a recent story on health plan liability in the August 1996 issue of *Medical Economics*,

> [M]any plaintiffs' attorneys find HMOs more compelling defendants than doctors: As big, impersonal corporations with 'deep pockets,' they're unlikely to evoke much sympathy from jurors. In fact, some lawyers will offer to settle or drop claims against treating physicians in exchange for their cooperation in a suit against a health plan.

LAWSUITS WILL NOT BENEFIT PATIENTS

Moreover, the bill creates the strongest possible incentive for plans to completely restructure their relationships with physicians. Under the bill, plans would find it essential to become directly involved in physician practices and treatment decisions. Ironically, then, a bill intended to promote physician autonomy would eliminate the very considerable autonomy that physicians have today.

The current medical liability system rightly has been criticized by physicians and others as inefficient, expensive, and frequently of little benefit to those who have been injured. According to a Rand Corporation study, only 43 cents of every dollar spent on medical liability litigation reaches injured patients as compensation. Moreover, the medical liability system has become an uncertain "litigation lottery" that too often fails to provide relief to injured patients who deserve compensation and inappropriately rewards those who do not. This is why virtually every state has limited access to the flawed medical malpractice system by enacting tort reform. Expanding state tort law to expose health plans, insurers, their employees, and employers who voluntarily sponsor health benefit plans to medical liability lawsuits will only make a flawed system worse.

LAWYER-SHY DOCTORS

Unlimited liability gets you more medicine, not better. Lawyer-shy doctors administer tests willy-nilly, and hand off patients to specialists with great alacrity. They know that the surest way to avoid liability is to dispatch your problem patient to someone else—a lab technician or another doctor. This can go on indefinitely. It's very expensive. And medically useless.

Peter Huber, *Forbes*, January 27, 1997.

New health plan medical liability litigation most certainly will bring with it a plethora of cases in which the very methods which have made health plans successful at delivering affordable, high quality care to Americans—methods such as quality assurance programs, utilization management, provider payment systems, and provider credentialing—are attacked as being the "proximate cause" of alleged injuries. Although in the end it is unlikely that such cases will be successful, the damage caused by increased litigation and other defensive costs arising from such cases will be irreparable.

This provision also will foster lawsuits whose sole purpose is to influence the range and scope of coverage provided by health plans and insurers. Instead of making medical appropriateness decisions based on scientific evidence and objective best practice protocols, health plans will be influenced to make these decisions based on the latest jury verdict or court decision in a medical liability case. Additionally, some may use aggressive litigation tactics as a way to circumvent coverage limitations clearly articulated in the language of the plan documents. This will undermine health plans' and employers' ability to contractually fix the range and scope of coverage to be provided and to control the costs associated with such coverage. Plan sponsors not permitted to determine the coverage they will voluntarily offer may withdraw coverage altogether.

As a result, in much the same way that physicians have been forced to practice "defensive medicine," health plans will be influenced to provide coverage for unnecessary services that do not benefit patients in order to avoid costly litigation. Moreover, physicians could be influenced to recommend treatments which may not benefit the patient, knowing that the onus will be on the health plan to cover the cost of the treatment or face a possible lawsuit. Again, although these types of lawsuits may fail ultimately, the cost of defending against them will be significant.

In contrast, because of the capricious nature of the medical liability system, few of the isolated individuals who may have sustained a personal injury as a result of actual negligence will be compensated. It is important to keep in mind that ERISA plan beneficiaries already have the right to seek to recover benefits they believe they are entitled to under the plan. Moreover, they need not wait for an injury to occur to seek recovery. An ERISA participant or beneficiary who believes that he or she has wrongfully been denied coverage of a benefit may seek injunctive relief in the form of a court order to have the benefit provided long before any injury is sustained.

THE WRONG ANSWER

In the end, the bill's liability provision will (1) expose patients to questionable care, (2) raise costs by undermining the cost containment mechanisms that have only recently brought health care expenditures under control, (3) reduce the availability of types of health plans that many patients have chosen, and (4) suppress new and better ways of organizing health coverage. Physicians still will be subject to suits. Employers and consumers will be forced to bear the brunt of the administrative cost increases associated with increased liability insurance and litigation. The health care system will become more adversarial, alienating consumers, health plans, and providers.

The Patient Access to Responsible Care Act's liability provision is quite simply the wrong answer to the concerns it is attempting to address. It overlooks the important role of current processes and requirements designed to deal with a problem at the "front end"—before errors are made and injuries are sustained.

Clearly, what is needed is expeditious, accessible processes for resolving disputes. A more appropriate means for meeting consumer needs than increased exposure to litigation is to ensure that patients have access to fast, fair, and efficient processes and procedures for resolving disputes or grievances about their health care. Health plans are committed to achieving this through effective quality improvement programs, accreditation, and risk management programs. Health plans are, right now, developing innovations for the grievances and appeals processes they are already required to have under state law.

BETTER WAYS OF RESOLVING DISPUTES

In addition to state regulatory requirements, AAHP member health plans have committed themselves . . . to appeals processes which provide timely notice to a patient when an adverse coverage recommendation is made and which include an easily understood description of the patient's appeal rights. Additionally, AAHP member plans are committed to providing an expedited appeals process when the normal time frames for an appeal could jeopardize a patient's life or health. . . . AAHP is currently working with member plans to identify "best practices" among internal plan processes for dispute resolution. Typically, health plans continually monitor and review their handling of disputes. In their efforts to minimize confusion, avoid conflicts, and resolve disputes promptly and fairly, a number of health plans are involved in active outreach to consumer advocates, state and federal regulators, and others with an interest in this issue.

Related to the appeals processes used by health plans . . . are new requirements emerging in a number of states for another level of review of health plan coverage determinations which is external to the health plan. These external review processes, if designed properly, may provide a further assurance to patients that the decisions made about their health care coverage are fair and being made based on scientific evidence and best practices.

> "The statistics on smoking, obesity, and vaccination rates are understandable to most people as legitimate health care–related concerns."

THE GOVERNMENT SHOULD ENCOURAGE HEALTHY BEHAVIOR

James Moore

In the following viewpoint, James Moore argues that a major problem with the health care system is that current policies do not hold people accountable for their poor health decisions. Moore proposes that the cost of a person's health insurance should be based on whether the person smokes, drinks, eats right, and exercises. He also believes that communities have a pivotal role in educating about healthful behavior, and that the federal government should set national health goals and set up a plan to meet them. James Moore is a physician at Butterworth General Hospital in Grand Rapids, Michigan, and codirector of the integrated health care program at Greenwich University in Hilo, Hawaii.

As you read, consider the following questions:

1. What are the "major determinants" that drive health, according to Tom Chapman, as quoted by the author?
2. According to Moore, what percent of health care expenditures go toward the medical costs associated with violent crime?
3. What are two of the goals that the government of Nova Scotia, Canada, hopes to reach by 2005?

Excerpted from James Moore, "Raising the Bar: Bringing Accountability to Health Care," *National Civic Review*, Spring 1997. Copyright 1997 Jossey-Bass Inc., Publishers. Reprinted with permission. *Endnote numbering has been changed from that in the original to match this reprint.*

It is almost fatiguing to think about the present state of health care in this country. The jumble of positioning, self-interests, conflicting approaches, and fuzzy goals appears to have mired us in a situation in which real progress is not only difficult to define but harder still to find. Americans—addicted to the quick fix and under increasing time pressures in their personal and work lives—have clung to a health care system that is largely reactive in nature. We apparently prefer to spend more money fixing problems as they arise than to spend less money and invest a little personal commitment up front to prevent problems. This approach keeps us focused on the manifestation of symptoms in individuals rather than the identification and elimination of causes of health care problems in the community. . . .

BROADER PERSPECTIVES

We think of health from a very narrow perspective. Instead of viewing illness as something predictable, preventable, and manageable, we typically view it as unpredictable and event-driven. Instead of developing a lifelong, low-intensity relationship with our clients, we interact with them only when a problem arises. Instead of measuring our success by the number of people in whom we have prevented illness, we measure it by the number of bodies that are in our custody on any given evening. We rarely embrace a wider definition of health that involves communities "empowering organizations at the local level" and "developing understanding of [the community's] interdependency."[1] Along this line, Tom Chapman, who is the former chief executive officer of Greater Southeast in Washington, D.C., and current head of George Washington University Medical Center, advocates for "a pure and thorough recognition that it is not health care delivery that fundamentally drives health. Other major determinants—such as good housing, jobs, a strong economic base, good nutrition, responsible behavior, genetic makeup, and education—dwarf health care. One of our frustrations as providers is that the harder we work to provide health, the further we get behind, because we have no influence over these other determinants. It doesn't work to use the term 'healthy community' in a narrow parochial sense. If everybody gets immunized but kids get blown away in gang warfare, that's not a healthy community."[2] Susan Sullivan, of the National Business Coalition, shares this perspective in noting that issues like crime, education, housing, or how the community feels about itself "are not things that usually show up in conversations of health care reformers about ways of reducing health care costs—or things that managed competition will have much impact on."[3]

Many defenders of the status quo would question my assertion that the system is not really working as well as it should be. "We have the best health care system in the world," some might argue. I agree that our technology is probably the best, and there are many aspects of our current system that I would not trade for any other. If I were involved in a major auto accident, for example, I would want to visit a level-3 trauma center and have a trained trauma team standing by. If I needed an emergency appendectomy, I would want it done in a surgical suite of a reputable hospital in the United States. But, from a broader perspective relating to the level of health experienced in our communities, the system does not always work as well as we would like to think.

THE SOBERING STATISTICS ON HEALTH VERSUS HEALTH CARE SPENDING

In fact, data from the National Center for Health Statistics[4] paint a grim picture: 31.2 percent of all high school seniors smoked cigarettes in the past month, up from 30.5 percent in 1980, and 18.6 percent of all eighth-graders smoked in the past month; 19 percent of all high school seniors and 7.8 percent of all eighth-graders smoked marijuana in the past month; 28.2 percent of all high school seniors and 14.5 percent of all eighth-graders participated in binge drinking in the past month; cocaine-related emergency room visits increased from 28,801 in 1985 to 123,317 in 1993, an astonishing fourfold increase in only eight years; the number of overweight persons from ages twenty to seventy-four, as a percentage of the population, has steadily increased from 24.4 percent in 1960–1962 to 33.3 percent in 1988–1991; in only three years, the total percentage of our national population who experience limitations of activity caused by chronic conditions increased from 12.9 percent to 14.6 percent; our inpatient and residential treatment episodes in mental health organizations increased from 1,817,000 in 1975 to 2,264,000 in 1991, an increase of 20 percent; only 67.1 percent of our children from the ages of nineteen to thirty-five months have received the standard combined series of four doses of DTP vaccine, three doses of polio vaccine, and one dose of measles vaccine; according to the Alan Guttmacher Institute, legal abortions increased from 616,000 per year in 1973 to 1,359,000 per year in 1992; the number of people living below the poverty line increased from 11.1 percent in 1973 to over 15 percent in 1993; death rates due to homicide have almost doubled from 5.4 deaths per 100,000 resident population in 1950 to 10.5 deaths per 100,000 resident population in 1990–1992. Moreover, we are experiencing increases in completely preventable and treatable diseases such as syphilis and tuberculosis. Fully one-third of our children have health-related problems that interfere with their ability to learn on the first day of kindergarten. In a survey[5] of forty industrialized nations that rated citizen satisfaction with their own health care system, the United States was ranked dead last. Infant mortality and male and female life-expectancy rates are near the bottom of the list when compared to the other developed nation members of the Organization for Economic Cooperation and Development (OECD). . . .

UNHEALTHY INDIVIDUALS THREATEN THE WELFARE OF SOCIETY

Despite the "pro-choice" arguments of, say, the National Smokers Alliance, I know of no claimed right of individuals to threaten the welfare of society by unhealthy behavior. Laws against spitting, urinating, and defecating in public places have public health as their principal goal, and are well accepted in all civilized societies. It is now time to move on to still more areas of private activity. Unhealthy private behavior, even if hidden from the public eye, can have equally harmful public consequences: excessive obesity and lack of exercise increase the health care costs of all, while teenage pregnancy generates myriad undesirable social and familial harms. For that matter, a person who lives an egregiously unhealthy private life is more likely to do harm to us (and his family) through his health care burdens and costs than someone who urinates on the sidewalk. It is cheaper to hose down a sidewalk than to subsidize ICU care.

In modern, interdependent societies, and in modern health care systems, where risks and costs are shared, the private realm quickly affects the public realm. Everything we do to ourselves behind closed doors, from sex to diet to exercise, will have a public impact. While it is difficult, in free societies, to find a legal or moral basis to coerce competent adults for their own good, it may be possible to make such a case on social grounds—that is, the effect of our unhealthy behavior on others, directly (as with passive smoke) or indirectly (shared community costs of health care).

Daniel Callahan, *False Hopes:Why America's Quest for Perfect Health Is a Recipe for Failure.*
New York: Simon & Schuster, 1998.

These figures document an abysmal overall track record considering the money we throw at health care every year in the United States. The dollars we are spending in health care should be giving us more bang for our buck. Health insurance as a percentage of total compensation packages for state and local government entities, for example, increased from 6.9 percent in 1991 to 8.2 percent in 1994.[6] The increase for private industry went from 6.0 percent to 6.7 percent for the same period. National health expenditures as a percentage of the gross domestic product rose from 5.3 percent in 1960 to 13.9 percent in 1993. Health care as a percentage of total federal government expenditures rose from 3.1 percent in 1960 to a shocking 18.6 percent in 1993. Per capita health expenditures are greater in the United States ($3,066) than in any of the other members of the OECD. The nearest competitor is Switzerland at $2,068. No other member even breaks the $2,000 mark. The consumer price index (CPI) rating for medical care in 1950 was 15.1, lower than that for food, apparel, housing, energy, or personal care. The sector closest to health care was food, which stood at 25.4. In 1994, the CPI rating for medical care was 211.0 and the closest rating was 144.8, which was for housing. Quite a reversal! If throwing money at the problem was the solution to improved health statistics, this nation should be almost disease- and injury-free. Instead, we have some of the worst health statistics among developed nations. If a student brought home the kind of grades on his or her report card that we should be getting on our health care report card, that student would be failing. In the cost-benefit ratio section of the national health care report card, we flunk hands-down.

THE MANY FACTORS THAT IMPACT HEALTH CARE

The statistics on smoking, obesity, and vaccination rates are understandable to most people as legitimate health care-related concerns. But many people have a problem linking such issues as crime, poverty, and pollution to health care. The most common response that I hear is something like the following: "I know those are important issues, but crime is the police department's problem, social services agencies need to deal with poverty and the Environmental Protection Agency should take care of the polluters."

Unfortunately, that is the kind of fragmented thinking that continues to thwart efforts to achieve real change and progress. Let us take violent crime as an example. Three percent of our health care costs in the United States are expended on treatment for victims of violent crime. Fourteen percent go toward "clean-up" medical costs associated with homicides, rapes, assaults, robberies, drunk driving, and domestic and child abuse. I often wonder what else we could do with this 17 percent of a $1.4 trillion national health care budget if we did not have to spend it on clean-up medical costs associated with crime.

No one can deny the health consequences related to smoking or drug use. The governor's budget summary for the state of California speaks of the devastating consequences of unwed mothers and teenage births.[7] This scenario, like the problems associated with obesity due to lack of exercise and overeating, and the problem of motor vehicle accidents due to drinking and driving, involves matters that often reflect poor personal choices and have the effect of diverting resources that are critically needed for other purposes.

The point is that health care is the lowest common denominator of a society. We can live without a lot of things but it is very difficult to live any kind of a quality life without good health. Therefore, we can no longer afford to argue about whose responsibility it is to take care of crime, poverty, and pollution or about the proposition that some of these issues are separate from others, or from health care. That approach is fallacious. These are all health care issues. And we had better start looking at them from the perspective of causal connections.

Where does accountability fit into the equation of bringing about real change? Quite simply, without the expectation for accountability on individual, community, and national levels, we have little hope of making any real progress.

HOLDING PEOPLE ACCOUNTABLE FOR THEIR HEALTH DECISIONS

Let us talk about individual accountability—about survey results indicating that 31 percent of high school students are smoking, about the fact that 19 percent of high school students have smoked marijuana in the past month, about the fact that 28 percent of high school students have been binge drinking in the past month, about how cocaine-related emergency room visits have increased fourfold in the past eight years, about how child abuse cases have increased 12.8 percent in only two years, about how the number of abortions has doubled to about 1,359,000 annually since 1973, about how births to unmarried women have exploded 67 percent since 1970, and about how one-third of our population is overweight. These are sensitive issues. They are personal in nature. It could be argued that some of these issues are of such a personal nature that they are inappropriate topics for a discussion on health care or personal accountability. After all, the right to smoke, to decide what and how much we eat, or to decide to have and how to raise children involves intensely personal decisions that should not be interfered with by others. I agree, but with the caveat that the individuals involved must be willing to pay the expenses associated with their decisions and not expect others to pick up the tab.

Personal accountability in health care means that people who make poor decisions about their life-styles—decisions that will adversely affect their health—must be willing to pay for those decisions. Nonsmokers, for example, should not be saddled with the additional expenses that smokers add to health care costs.

One way to promote accountability is to base premium costs and the amount of employees' contributions to their health care plans on life-styles. People should not, of course, be penalized for preexisting conditions. But such factors as smoking, drinking, driving habits, nutritional and exercise patterns, and cholesterol levels can be measured and used to determine employee contribution levels to health care premium costs. This makes people shareholders in their health care coverage plan. When people are absolved of any responsibility for personal actions that impact finances, they tend not to make the same decisions that they would make if they were held accountable for consequences. I believe health care costs could immediately be reduced and health statistics improved if a component of personal responsibility were built into premium structures.

PROMOTING COMMUNITY HEALTH

Community accountability is ultimately based on a recognition that the federal and state governments are not in a position to adequately address regional health care needs. President Clinton's attempt to reform health care failed largely because there was the recognition that a federal system could not be applied to the unique needs of individual communities. Even states were not seen as able to create such a system. Communities on the southeastern side of Michigan, for example, have much different needs than communities on the Lake Michigan shoreline. In a state-designed system, one of these communities would have likely emerged as a winner and the other a loser.

As a result, individual communities across the country began developing their own plans. . . .

In a small town in North Carolina, the citizens converted a potato shack into a health clinic and taught themselves how to screen for diabetes and improve their nutritional habits. They instituted exercise programs and learned how to reduce their intake of fried foods. They battled the large commercial stock farms that were polluting the environment and threatening their children's health. The results include dramatically lower heart disease and cancer rates and a better understanding of how to deal with diabetes.

Addressing causes rather than symptoms—although sometimes a complicated and controversial undertaking—appears to be a better approach from the perspective of cost containment, and it is certainly a better deal if we consider quality of life. In other words, the cost-benefit analysis in general appears to support prevention rather than intervention after disease or injury manifests. This is both a shared responsibility and a shared opportunity for individuals and the larger community.

Dean Ornish, for example, has developed a program using exercise, meditation, group support, and dietary changes that not only can stop the development of heart disease but actually reverse it. So compelling are the results that major insurance companies are reimbursing for the program. The benefits are clear—heart bypass surgery can cost upward of $50,000 but does not really address the source of the disease. Ornish's program costs around $5,000 and it gets to the cause. Spending less on expensive surgery as a result of the individual making responsible life-style choices is a benefit for both the individual and the community. The individual improves his or her quality of life and the community reduces health care costs or reallocates precious resources. . . .

A Systems Issue

Many—possibly most—physical disorders have a major psychological factor. It can be far cheaper to help someone rethink his or her life than to use medicine to "fix" them. Yet, insurance companies usually highly restrict the coverage for psychological counseling, dietary education, and life-style "fixes"—anything even remotely outside the medical diagnose-dose-cut model.

We need to understand that health care cannot be approached from the perspective of fragmentation. It must be approached with sensitivity to the fact that it is a systems issue. As a systems issue, it is automatically a communal issue. All the facets that impact the traditional definition of health care—including crime, economics, housing, pollution, workplace safety, child care, education, and agriculture—are part-and-parcel of health care. That means that causal effects in both the individual and the community must be of primary concern and must be addressed in a coordinated manner.

Lee Kaiser talks about the auto repair shop metaphor for health care. A person wears out his car's brakes prematurely and goes to the repair shop, and they replace his brakes. Nobody ever talks to him about why his brakes are not lasting as long as they should because he is riding them constantly or using them incorrectly. We need to explain to the man that he cannot abuse his brakes and expect them to last. But we also need to explore why he is abusing them. Otherwise we replace the parts without correcting the problem. Perhaps riding his brakes is an expression of stress due to family tension, work problems, or depression. We can expect him to be in again for repair work unless we help him with these issues.

It is impossible to separate the accountability of the individual and that of the community when examining the issue of health care. The community simply reflects the sum total of all individuals. They cannot be pulled apart. There are parallels to this concept in all major spiritual traditions. The basic oneness of the universe is not only the central characteristic of the mystical experience but also one of the most important revelations of modern physics.[8] In various models of subatomic physics, the constituents of matter and the basic phenomena involving them are all interconnected, interrelated, and interdependent. They cannot be understood as isolated entities but only as integrated parts of the whole.

MAKING GOVERNMENT MORE RESPONSIBLE

The interrelatedness of individual and community expands to national, global, and universal levels and involves responsibility at each level. Individuals cannot say that "government is responsible to solve the problem." Government cannot say that "individuals must solve the problem."

But I must say that the federal government, like many individuals, has done a less than stellar job of holding itself responsible for offering workable, real-life answers to many of the problems faced in this country, health care included. The standard answer has been to throw money at problems. Comparing health statistics with dollars spent shows that this practice is unworkable. It has also resulted in a national debt that threatens the security of our children's future.

The government must be held to the same standard that I have proposed for individuals and communities. That is the identification of issues and the establishment of specific goals and time frames by which success can be measured. From this perspective, we could learn something from the government of Nova Scotia. The government has started a process to develop and adopt measures that monitor its progress as a province, setting its sights on an ambitious list of goals. These goals include increasing the percentage of the population who are nonsmokers from 66 percent in 1994 to 77 percent in 2005; reducing deaths (per 100,000 people) from lung cancer from 48.4 in 1994 to 46 in 2005, heart disease from 165 in 1994 to 120 in 2005, respiratory disease from 50.7 in 1994 to 48 in 2005; reducing the average number of prescriptions necessary for seniors each year from twenty-four in 1994 to fifteen in 2005; reducing the number of institutional admissions for substance abuse (per 100,000 people) from 104 in 1994 to 34 in 2005; increasing the number of children who are immunized from 90 percent in 1994 to 99 percent in 2005; reducing the number of teen pregnancies (ages fifteen to nineteen) per 1,000 live births from 45.4 in 1994 to 36 in 2005; reducing the number of young offenders charged from 4,372 in 1994 to 4,000 in 2005; and reducing patient days per 1,000 population from 1,200 in 1994 to 800 in 2005.

Nova Scotia may not achieve all of these goals. But the provincial government has taken a critical first step by analyzing needs, establishing targets, and setting up a plan to meet them. In the next several years the government can gauge its success or failure by referring back to the goals it set out to accomplish.

RESTORING RESPONSIBILITY TO HEALTH CARE

We seem to have developed a general trend toward the absence of responsibility in our society. That may be a dangerous thing to say. But I really believe that many Americans feel that, in general, people are not truly held accountable for their actions. I am not talking about extreme political or judicial stances here. I am talking about reasonable expectations that people be willing to bear the consequences of their decisions, participate in a useful sense within the community, and contribute toward creating a better society.

If we hope to get our arms around the issues of escalating costs, poor health statistics, questionable outcomes, and deteriorating living conditions, we must restore the elements of personal, community, and national accountability and commitment. This can be done in many ways that preserve dignity, individualism, and concern for others. But it must be done now.

NOTES

1. Flower, J. *The Revolution in Our Assumptions About Healthcare:* Brighton, Colo.: HealthOnLine; Leland Kaiser, Sept. 6, 1996 (accessed).
2. Flower, J. *How to Build a Health Community.* Brighton, Colo.: HealthOnLine; Leland Kaiser, Sept. 6, 1996 (accessed).

3. Flower, J. *How to Build a Health Community.* Brighton, Colo.: HealthOnLine; Leland Kaiser, Sept. 6, 1996 (accessed).

4. National Center for Health Statistics, *Health, United States.* Hayattsville, Md.: Public Health Service, 1994.

5. Flower, J. *Simulating a Healthcare System That Works.* Brighton, Colo.: HealthOnLine; Leland Kaiser, Sept. 6, 1996 (accessed).

6. National Center for Health Statistics, 1994.

7. Governor's Budget Summary. *The Prevention Agenda: A Partnership for Responsible Parenting and a Healthier California.* Sacramento, Calif., Oct. 18, 1996.

8. Capra, F. *The Tao of Physics.* Boston: Shambala, 1988.

> *"A government empowered to maximize health is a totalitarian government."*

THE GOVERNMENT SHOULD NOT REGULATE BEHAVIOR

Jacob Sullum

Jacob Sullum is senior editor of *Reason* magazine and the author of *For Your Own Good: The Anti-Smoking Crusade and the Tyranny of Public Health*, from which the following viewpoint is excerpted. In it, he argues that public health advocates have classified many risky behaviors, such as smoking or eating fatty foods, as diseases: compulsive behaviors that the government should try to change. From a public health perspective, says Sullum, an individual's health decisions affect the health care system and society as a whole. Sullum warns that this argument—that unhealthy people harm society by raising health care costs—could be used to justify government control of all behaviors that affect health.

As you read, consider the following questions:

1. What reasons did the National Institutes of Health cite in their declaration that obesity is a disease, according to the March 1985 *Science* article that Sullum quotes?
2. Why does the author believe that a "fat tax" is ridiculous?
3. In Sullum's opinion, what important distinction does former surgeon general C. Everett Koop ignore in his defense of government public health policies?

Reprinted with the permission of The Free Press, a division of Simon & Schuster, Inc., from *For Your Own Good: The Anti-Smoking Crusade and the Tyranny of Public Health*, by Jacob Sullum. Copyright ©1998 by Jacob Sullum. Endnotes in the original have been omitted in this reprint.

Public health used to mean keeping statistics, imposing quarantines, requiring vaccination of children, providing purified water, building sewer systems, inspecting restaurants, regulating emissions from factories, and reviewing drugs for safety. Nowadays it means, among other things, banning cigarette ads, raising alcohol taxes, restricting gun ownership, forcing people to buckle their seat belts, and making illegal drug users choose between prison and "treatment." In the past, public health officials could argue that they were protecting people from external threats: carriers of contagious diseases, fumes from the local glue factory, contaminated water, food poisoning, dangerous quack remedies. By contrast, the new enemies of public health come from within; the aim is to protect people from themselves rather than each other.

Treating risky behavior like a contagious disease invites endless meddling. The same arguments that are commonly used to justify the government's efforts to discourage smoking can easily be applied to overeating, for example. If smoking is a compulsive disease, so is obesity. It carries substantial health risks, and people who are fat generally don't want to be. They find it difficult to lose weight, and when they do succeed they often relapse. When deprived of food, they suffer cravings, depression, anxiety, and other withdrawal symptoms.

Obesity as a Disease

Sure enough, the headline of a March 1985 article in *Science* announced, "Obesity Declared a Disease." The article summarized a report by a National Institutes of Health panel that found that "the obese are prone to a wide variety of diseases, including hypertension, adult-onset diabetes, hypercholesterolemia, hypertriglyceridemia, heart disease, cancer, gall stones, arthritis, and gout." It quoted the panel's chairman, Jules Hirsch: "We found that there are multiple health hazards at what to me are surprisingly low levels of obesity. Obesity, therefore, is a disease."

More recently, the "epidemic of obesity" has been trumpeted repeatedly on the front page of the *New York Times*. The first story, which appeared in July 1994, was prompted by a study from the National Center for Health Statistics that found the share of American adults who are obese increased from a quarter to a third between 1980 and 1991. "The government is not doing enough," complained Philip R. Lee, assistant HHS secretary. "We don't have a coherent, across-the-board policy." The second story, published in September 1995, reported on a *New England Journal of Medicine* study that found gaining as little as eleven to eighteen pounds was associated with a higher risk of heart disease—or, as the headline on the jump page put it, EVEN MODERATE WEIGHT GAINS CAN BE DEADLY. The study attributed three hundred thousand deaths a year to obesity, including one-third of cancer deaths and most deaths from cardiovascular disease. The lead researcher, JoAnn E. Manson, said, "It won't be long before obesity surpasses cigarette smoking as a cause of death in this country."

In his book *The Fat of the Land*, journalist Michael Fumento argues that obesity, defined as being 20 percent or more above one's appropriate weight, is only part of the problem. According to a 1996 survey, 74 percent of Americans exceed the weight range recommended for optimal health. "So instead of talking about a third of Americans being at risk because of being overweight," he writes, "we really should be talking about somewhere around *three fourths*."

A FAT TAX

If, as Philip R. Lee recommended, the government decides to do more about obesity—the second most important preventable cause of death in this country, soon to be the first—what would "a coherent, across-the-board policy" look like? As early as June 1975, in its *Forward Plan for Health*, the U.S. Public Health Service was suggesting "strong regulations to control the advertisement of food products, especially those of high sugar content or little nutritional value." But surely we can do better than that. A tax on fatty foods would help cover the cost of obesity-related illness and disability, while deterring overconsumption of ice cream and steak.

Lest you think this proposal merely facetious, it has been offered, apparently in all seriousness, by at least one economist, who wrote: "It is somewhat ironic that the government discourages smoking and drinking through taxation, yet when it comes to the major cause of death—heart disease—and its spiraling health-care costs, politicians let us eat with impunity. . . . It is time to rethink the extent to which we allow people to impose their negative behavior on those of us who watch our weight, exercise and try to be as healthy as possible."

Kelly Brownell, a professor of psychology at Yale University who directs the school's Center for Eating and Weight Disorders, has also suggested a fat tax, along with subsidies for healthy foods. "A militant attitude is warranted here," he told the *New Haven Register*. "We're infuriated at tobacco companies for enticing kids to smoke, so we don't want Joe Camel on billboards. Is it any different to have Ronald McDonald asking kids to eat foods that are bad for them?"

Of course, a tax on fatty foods would be paid by the lean as well as the chunky. It might be more fair and efficient to tax people for every pound over their ideal weight. Such a market-based system would make the obese realize the costs they impose on society and give them an incentive to slim down.

STATE INTRUSION INTO PRIVATE MATTERS

If this idea strikes most people as ridiculous, it's not because the plan is impractical. In several states, people have to bring their cars to an approved garage for periodic emissions testing; there's no logistical reason why they could not also be required to weigh in at an approved doctor's office, say, once a year, reporting the results to the Internal Revenue Service for tax assessment. Though feasible, the fat tax is ridiculous because it's an odious intrusion by the state into matters that should remain private. Even if obesity is apt to shorten your life, most Americans would (I hope) agree, that's your business, not the government's. . . .

SOCIETAL NEEDS VS. INDIVIDUAL RIGHTS

The consensus appears to be that public health could use a little more "balance" and "moderation." That is encouraging as far as it goes, but it is also worrisome. I picture a bunch of technocrats weighing the costs and benefits of each policy (including, of course, its impact on individual freedom) and deciding whether it's justified: cigarette ban, no; handgun ban, yes; fat tax, no; helmet law, yes. If the government gets to decide, on a case-by-case basis, when the needs of "society" override individual rights, those rights are not very meaningful.

Jacob Sullum, *Reason*, April 1996.

Because the public health field developed in response to deadly threats that spread from person to person and place to place, its practitioners are used to dictating from on high. Writing in 1879, U.S. Army surgeon John S. Billings put it this way: "All admit that the State should extend special protection to those who are incapable of judging their own best interests, or of taking care of themselves, such as the insane, persons of feeble intellect, or children; and we have seen that in sanitary matters the public at large are thus incompetent." Billings was defending traditional public health measures aimed at preventing the spread of infectious diseases and controlling hazards such as toxic fumes. It's reasonable to expect that such measures will be welcomed by the intended beneficiaries, once they understand the aim. The same cannot be said of public health's new targets. Even after the public is informed about the relevant hazards (and assuming the information is accurate), many people will continue to smoke, drink, take illegal drugs, eat fatty foods, buy guns, speed, eschew seat belts and motorcycle helmets, and otherwise behave in ways frowned upon by the public health establishment. This is not because they misunderstood; it's because, for the sake of pleasure, utility, or convenience, they are prepared to accept the risks. When public health experts assume these decisions are wrong, they are indeed treating adults like incompetent children.

AN OVERLY BROAD DEFINITION OF PUBLIC HEALTH

One such expert, writing in the *New England Journal of Medicine* two decades ago, declared, "The real malpractice problem in this country today is not the one described on the front pages of daily newspapers but rather the malpractice that people are performing on themselves and each other—It is a crime to commit suicide quickly. However, to kill oneself slowly by means of an unhealthy life style is readily condoned and even encouraged." The article prompted a response from Robert F. Meenan, a professor at the University of California School of Medicine in San Francisco, who observed: "Health professionals are trained to supply the individual with medical facts and opinions. However, they have no personal attributes, knowledge, or training that qualifies them to dictate the preferences of others. Nevertheless, doctors generally assume that the high priority that they place on health should be shared by others. They find it hard to accept that some people may opt for a brief, intense existence full of unhealthy practices. Such individuals are pejoratively labeled 'noncompliant' and pressures are applied on them to reorder their priorities."

The dangers of basing government policy on this attitude are clear, especially given the broad concerns of the public health movement. According to John J. Hanlon's *Public Health Administration and Practice*, "Public health is dedicated to the common attainment of the highest levels of physical, mental, and social well-being and longevity consistent with available knowledge and resources at a given time and place." The textbook *Principles of Community Health* tells us, "The most widely accepted definition of individual health is that of the World Health Organization: 'Health is a state of complete physical, mental, and social well-being and not merely the absence of disease or infirmity.'" A government empowered to maximize health is a totalitarian government.

"Crimes Against Society"

In response to such fears, the public health establishment argues that government intervention is justified because individual decisions about risk affect other people. "Motorcyclists often contend that helmet laws infringe on personal liberties," noted Surgeon General Julius Richmond's 1979 report *Healthy People*, "and opponents of mandatory [helmet] laws argue that since other people usually are not endangered, the individual motorcyclist should be allowed personal responsibility for risk. But the high cost of disabling and fatal injuries, the burden on families, and the demands on medical care resources are borne by society as a whole." This line of reasoning, which is also used to justify taxes on tobacco and alcohol, implies that all resources—including not just taxpayer-funded welfare and health care but private savings, insurance coverage, and charity—are part of a common pool owned by "society as a whole" and guarded by the government.

As Meenan noted in the *New England Journal of Medicine*, "Virtually all aspects of life style could be said to have an effect on the health or well-being of society, and the decision [could then be] reached that personal health choices should be closely regulated." Writing eighteen years later in the same journal, Faith T. Fitzgerald, a professor at the University of California, Davis, Medical Center, observed: "Both health care providers and the commonweal now have a vested interest in certain forms of behavior, previously considered a person's private business, if the behavior impairs a person's 'health.' Certain failures of self-care have become, in a sense, crimes against society, because society has to pay for their consequences. . . . In effect, we have said that people owe it to society to stop misbehaving, and we use illness as evidence of misbehavior."

A Dangerous Argument

Most public health practitioners would presumably recoil at the full implications of the argument that government should override individual decisions affecting health because such decisions have an impact on "society as a whole." C. Everett Koop, for his part, seems completely untroubled. "I think that the government has a perfect right to influence personal behavior to the best of its ability if it is for the welfare of the individual and the community as a whole," he writes. This is paternalistic tyranny in its purest form, arrogating to government the authority to judge "the welfare of the individual" and elevating "the community as a whole" above mere people. Ignoring the distinction between self-regarding behavior and behavior that threatens others, Koop compares efforts to discourage smoking and other risky behavior to mandatory vaccination of schoolchildren and laws against assault.

While Koop may simply be confused, some defenders of the public health movement explicitly recognize that its aims are fundamentally collectivist and cannot be reconciled with the American tradition of limited government. In 1975 Dan E. Beauchamp, then an assistant professor of public health at the University of North Carolina, presented a paper at the annual meeting of the American Public Health Association in which he argued that "the radical individualism inherent in the market model" is the biggest obstacle to improving public health. "The historic dream of public health that preventable death and disability ought to be minimized is a dream of social justice," Beauchamp said. "We are far from recognizing the principle that death and disability are collective problems and that all persons are entitled to health protection." He rejected "the ultimately arbitrary distinction between voluntary and involuntary hazards" and complained that "the primary duty to avert disease and injury still rests with the individual." Beauchamp called upon public health practitioners to challenge "the powerful sway market-justice holds over our imagination, granting fundamental freedom to all individuals to be left alone."

Of all the risk factors for disease and injury, it seems, freedom is the most pernicious.

Periodical Bibliography

The following articles have been selected to supplement the diverse views presented in this chapter. Addresses are provided for periodicals not indexed in the *Readers' Guide to Periodical Literature*, the *Alternative Press Index*, the *Social Sciences Index*, or the *Index to Legal Periodicals and Books*.

Catherine Arnst and Stephanie Forest	"Are HMOs Crying Wolf? They Say Costs Will Soar if Patients Can Sue Them," *Business Week*, August 3, 1998.
Karlyn Bowman	"Patients Don't Want Protection from Their HMOs," *Wall Street Journal*, May 11, 1998.
Shannon Brownlee	"Trials of a Cancer Doc," *U.S. News & World Report*, October 5, 1998.
CQ Researcher	"Patients' Rights," February 6, 1998. Available from Congressional Quarterly, 1414 22nd St. NW, Washington, DC 20037.
Kim Erickson	"The Great Supplement Scare: Belief That Codex Commission and FDA Threaten Herbal Medicine," *E:The Environmental Magazine*, May/June 1998.
John Greenwald	"Herbal Healing," *Time*, November 23, 1998.
James O. Hill and John C. Peters	"Environmental Contributions to the Obesity Epidemic," *Science*, May 29, 1998.
Karen Ignagni	"Do Not Retard Progress," *USA Today*, July 13, 1998.
David Nather	"Protecting the Patient," *Washington Monthly*, July/August 1998.
Charlie Norwood	"Restoring Responsibility to Managed Care," *USA Today*, July 1998.
Robert M. Pear	"Senators Reject Bill to Regulate Care by H.M.O.'s," *New York Times*, October 9, 1998.
Ralph R. Reiland	"Joe Camel Today, the Pillsbury Doughboy Tomorrow," *Humanist*, July/August 1998.
Hanna Rosin	"The Fat Tax," *New Republic*, May 18, 1998.
Ellyn Spragins	"To Sue or Not to Sue?" *Newsweek*, December 9, 1996.
Jacob Sullum	"What the Doctor Orders: How the Public Health Lobby Prescribes Morality," *Reason*, January 1996.
William Tucker	"ERISA: A Prescription for Health Care Inequity," *American Spectator*, November 1998.
Karen Tumulty	"Let's Play Doctor," *Time*, July 13, 1998.

CHAPTER 4

HOW SHOULD THE UNITED STATES REFORM ITS HEALTH CARE SYSTEM?

CHAPTER PREFACE

Insurance is a means of guarding against life's uncertainties. Fire insurance is a basic example—homeowners make payments to their insurance company and, in the event of a fire, the insurance company pays for the damages. Most people pay more for the insurance than they ever collect in damages; this is how insurers make a profit. However, not purchasing fire insurance is generally considered a riskier gamble, since a fire, like an injury or illness, can be financially devastating.

But while most buildings are at roughly the same risk for fire, health varies a lot from person to person. Many factors—such as growing old, smoking, or being born into a family with a history of heart disease—increase a person's chances of having health problems. Robert Kuttner, editor of the *American Prospect*, believes the purpose of insurance is to spread these health risks across the population: "The young, who on average need little care, subsidize the old. The well subsidize the sick."

However, people buy insurance to protect themselves, not to subsidize others. Thus, many healthy young people choose to forego health insurance, waiting until they are more likely to experience health problems. This simple phenomenon is called "adverse selection," and it harms the insurance system, since it results in fewer healthy people paying premiums and more sick people filing claims. To help deal with this problem, insurers charge higher premiums to high-risk individuals, such as the elderly or people with chronic ailments, in order to offset the added costs they represent.

Paradoxically, then, the more a person needs health insurance, the less affordable it is. Kuttner believes this goes against the purpose of insurance and results in private insurers covering only the healthiest, leaving the government to care for the elderly and the poor with programs like Medicare and Medicaid. But insurers insist they must be able to charge higher premiums for people with adverse health conditions. As Jonathan Cohn, executive editor of the *New Republic*, explains, "If they couldn't charge more for consumers with pre-existing conditions, it would destroy the whole insurance system, since people would never buy insurance until they got sick."

The problem of adverse selection plagues health care reform as well, since, as the viewpoints in this chapter will show, health care reform is really health insurance reform. Each of the authors in this chapter is concerned with how accessible and affordable health insurance is, and what the government's role in health insurance should be.

"Canadians are endeavouring to develop a health care system directed at health needs—not a competitive system to serve an illness market."

CANADA'S SYSTEM IS A MODEL FOR HEALTH CARE REFORM

Pat Armstrong and Hugh Armstrong

In the following viewpoint, Pat and Hugh Armstrong, the authors of *Universal Health Care: What the United States Can Learn from the Canadian Experience*, argue that the Canadian system of national health insurance (known as medicare, with a small "m") is superior to the United States' market-based system. The Canadian system, they say, successfully provides quality health care to all Canadians, more efficiently and inexpensively than the U.S. system does. The Armstrongs contend that health care is very similar in both countries, but because no one is left uninsured under the Canadian system, it is a source of national pride for Canadians and a model for health care reform in other nations.

As you read, consider the following questions:

1. What are the five principles of the Canada Health Care Act?
2. What do the authors mean by the term "one-tier system"?
3. According to Pat and Hugh Armstrong, what percent of Canadians prefer their system to America's?

Ask any Canadian, "What is the difference between Canada and the United States?" Virtually every one of them will say "health care."

A remarkable 96 percent of Canadians prefer their health care system to the U.S. model. And this support is not simply a reflection of Canadian nationalism in the face of a very large neighbor, although medicare certainly plays a central role as a "defining national characteristic." Over the years, poll after poll has repeatedly demonstrated that health care is Canada's best-loved social program. An overwhelming majority of Canadians persistently say they want to keep their health care system.

In 1994, the Canadian government appointed a National Forum on Health to examine the current state and future possibilities of the health system. The focus groups and surveys conducted by the forum found that "the provision of health care services continues to receive strong and passionate support" among Canadians. Similarly, the president of a major polling firm reported recently that among government programs "only the health care system received approval from a majority of Canadians." He went on to point out that the support even crosses social class lines. Otherwise strong differences in class values "don't occur to the same extent in the area of health care, perhaps because everyone can see themselves as becoming sick at some point."

The current system is so popular that all Canadian politicians represent themselves as defenders of this sacred trust. Perhaps more surprisingly, so do many corporations in the private sector. Indeed, a major health insurance company has declared in a recent advertisement that it "believes strongly in the sanctity of Canadian medicare."

The most important explanation for this support can be found in what are known as the five principles of the Canada Health Act. These are criteria for funding set out by the federal government, criteria the provinces must follow in order to receive financial support for their health care services. Simply put, these principles require that core medical services be universal, portable, accessible, comprehensive, and publicly administered. In other words, all Canadians must have access to the medical services they require. These services must include all that is medically necessary, and must be provided regardless of age, prior condition, location, or employment. And they must be provided without regard to ability to pay. Canadian medicare was designed to allocate care on the basis of need, not individual finances.

And it worked. The system has delivered on the promised access to care. While "the number of uninsured Americans had risen to more than 40 million" in 1995, virtually every Canadian is covered for essential care. This contrast in access to care can be traced to the basic philosophical approach used to fund services in Canada. As one 1981 task force put it, "Canadians are endeavouring to develop a health care system directed at health needs—not a competitive system to serve an illness market."

This is made possible by the single-payer system. For the most part, health care in Canada is not *provided* by the government. It is *paid* for by governments. It is a public insurance system, a system in which governments at various levels pay for health services. Most of these services themselves are provided by nonprofit organizations or by doctors working on a fee-for-service basis. It is public payment for private practice and private provision. This single-payer system has made care in Canada cheaper than in the United States, both because it significantly reduces administrative costs and because it allows for more coherent management of services.

Until medicare was introduced, Canadian health care costs were growing as fast as those in the United States. But "the period of the most rapid escalation *ended* with the establishment of universal coverage" paid for from public funds. Even more startling is the fact that *public* spending on health care accounts for virtually the same proportion of each country's total economy. Yet, Canada covers the whole population and the United States covers only the elderly, the very poor, the military, and some of the disabled.

With the government as the main purchaser of services, health care is not only cheaper for individual taxpayers. It is also cheaper for employers, especially for those employers facing unions strong enough to successfully demand full health care coverage. In the United States, Chrysler pays more for health care than it pays for steel. In Canada, Chrysler does not have to pay for basic hospital or medical costs and therefore its employee costs are lower. Workers' compensation in Canada does not have to cover these basic costs either, and thus this protection too is cheaper for the Canadian employer.

With the single-payer scheme for many essential services, Canadians have a one-tier system. The rich and the poor go to the same hospitals and doctors. Neither receives a bill and the rich cannot buy quicker access, preferred status, or better facilities. What is covered by the public insurance system cannot be covered by a private insurer and doctors are not allowed to bill above the prescribed rate for services covered by the public insurance. Sharing facilities and services means that the entire population has a vested interest in maintaining the quality of care.

Tom Tomorrow, ©1998. Reprinted with permission.

For more than a quarter century, Canada has been providing this comprehensive, accessible and high-quality care, without billing individuals for services or relating care to financial status. Equally important, it has done so more efficiently and at least as effectively as the competitive system serving an illness market in the United States. It is not surprising, then, that 96 per cent of Canadians prefer their system to the American way. It is somewhat more surprising that a majority of Americans also prefer the Canadian system to that in the United States. After all, health care services are very similar on both sides of the border.

In both countries, hospitals form the core of the system. And an operating room in one country looks much like one in the other. Hospitals in both countries offer high-tech services. On both sides of the border, most hospitals are owned by non-government organizations and function largely as independent entities. Hospitals in both countries vary in size and degree of specialization, although teaching hospitals across the continent tend to be large and diverse. Once in the door, it would be difficult to tell Toronto Hospital from the hospital in *Chicago Hope*.

Similarly, it would be difficult to identify which doctors are Canadian and which are American. Not only do both kinds wear white coats and stethoscopes, but the majority of doctors are paid on a fee-for-service basis. They are formally governed by agencies primarily made up of peers, intended to protect both patients and providers. Across North America, specialties are very similar and so are medical techniques. Indeed, research is freely shared and even jointly conducted across the border. Like hospitals, doctors' offices look virtually the same in Canada and the United States. Marcus Welby could be a Canadian.

Although doctors in both countries have fought hard to gain a monopoly over diagnosis and other medical practices, most of the actual patient care is provided by nurses of various kinds. Even the categories of nurses are basically the same on both sides of the border, as is their range of skills. Nurses are the main care providers both in and out of the hospital setting.

The settings where nurses and others provide care include long-term care facilities of various sorts. Homes for the elderly, nursing homes, and group homes are common everywhere in North America. And in both countries a great deal of care is provided in the home, often with assistance from home care nurses or other aides.

If health care is so similar in both countries, why is there such a strong preference for the Canadian system evident across the border as well as at home? Again, the explanation can be found mainly in the five principles on which Canadian health care delivery is based [universal, portable, accessible, comprehensive, publicly administered health care]. And these in turn are related to the single-payer system and the insistence on one-tier delivery. They offer the most likely reasons for both Canadians and Americans preferring the Canadian approach.

"The hard truth is that socialized
medicine is destroying health care in
Canada."

CANADA'S SYSTEM IS NOT A MODEL
FOR HEALTH CARE REFORM

Michael J. Hurd

In the following viewpoint, Michael J. Hurd maintains that the
Canadian health care system has reduced the quality of health
care in Canada. Moreover, Hurd warns that the United States has
incorporated many of Canada's socialist principles into its health
care system, putting control of medical decisions in the hands
of HMOs and government bureaucracies rather than patients.
Health care, he argues, should be reformed according to the
principles of capitalism, not socialism. Michael J. Hurd is a psy-
chologist and the author of the books *Effective Therapy* and the
report *The Economic Effects of Aging in the United States and Japan*.

As you read, consider the following questions:
1. What is the wait for heart bypass surgery in Canada,
   according to the author?
2. According to Hurd, how many Canadian doctors fled to the
   United States in 1996?
3. What issue does the author say Canadians are divided over?

Reprinted from Michael J. Hurd, "Loved to Death: America's Unresolved Health Care
Crisis," *The Freeman*, November 1997, by permission of *The Freeman*.

The Canadian health-care system of single-payer, socialized insurance is in trouble. Yet Congress and the president continue to push the American system in the same direction.

As Canada's national government slashes spending on medical care in order to reduce the deficit, local provinces are reducing medical staff. In Ontario, pregnant women are being sent to Detroit because no obstetricians are available. Specialists of all kinds are in short supply. Patients have to wait eight weeks for an MRI, ten weeks for referral to a specialist, and four months for heart bypass surgery.

Does this sound like the utopian care Canadian politicians promised their constituents? The hard truth is that socialized medicine is destroying health care in Canada.

Loving Us to Death

Most Americans do not understand that we are headed down a similar path in this country. The same mistaken economic and philosophical ideas that created socialized medicine in Canada are leading to semi-socialized medicine in the United States. The increase in managed care, bureaucracy, waiting lists, and expense is largely the fault of the government. In its zeal to "compassionately" meet all of our health-care demands, the government is loving us to death.

How? First, the government pays, through Medicare and Medicaid, over 40 percent of all health-care expenditures. This massive infusion of cash into what were originally unregulated fee-for-service programs fueled demand for medical services, and thus inflated prices. Second, Washington allows tax write-offs to businesses for health insurance, but does not tax workers for the benefits. Consequently, employers have tended to provide comprehensive insurance.

Thus the vast majority of health care is paid for by a third party. Doctors do not have to worry if they are charging too much; the health insurance company (or the government, in the case of the elderly and poor) will pick up the tab. Patients do not have to shop carefully based on prices. Imagine if a third party picked up the tab for any other commodity—such as groceries, rent, television sets, or automobiles. Prices would skyrocket because the consumer would feel no pressure to spend carefully.

While the insurance companies and government, which are paying the bill, cannot shop for the consumer, they can place controls on the patient's freedom of choice. In the 1980s, Medicare officials began to set price controls ("Diagnostic Related Groups," or DRGs) on treatments for the elderly. In the 1990s private health insurance companies followed suit, by expanding Health Maintenance Organizations (HMOs) and other forms of managed care that often arbitrarily decide who may and may not receive treatment. Yet there was no alternative to such cost-saving steps, since without some kind of controls the price of medicine would rise ever higher. In that case there would have been pressure on the government to take over altogether, yielding something akin to the Canadian system: monopolistic, post office-style medical care.

Yet the growth of managed care has resulted in American patients encountering problems similar to those faced by Canadians—waiting lists for appointments, arbitrary treatment decisions made by bureaucrats rather than by physicians, and new price and treatment controls in government programs such as Medicare. Today the United States teeters on the brink of a Canadian-like system.

A Free Market in Medicine: The Unknown Ideal

How did we get to this point? And, more importantly, how can we reverse course and prevent a plunge into the disaster that Canada now faces? The answer is real capitalism.

Patients would be free to pursue any treatment they wanted. They would also be responsible for payment, encouraging them to select the best price available among competing medical providers and hospital insurance carriers.

Doctors and hospitals would be free to charge what they believed their services were worth; but they would also have to compete in a marketplace where they risked losses if they charged significantly more than their competitors or more than what most people were willing to pay. Patients, shopping as informed consumers in the marketplace, would do the cost-cutting that the HMOs and government bureaucrats currently do far less efficiently. Just as capitalism (or, more specifically, the law of supply and demand) succeeds in making food, computers, and other goods widely available at prices everyone can afford, so too with medicine and hospitalization insurance—if only the government would get out of the way and let the marketplace work.

The basic principles of economics would work no differently in the medical marketplace than in any other. The fact that medical treatment can be a matter of life or death does not prevent economic principles from operating. On the contrary, the life-or-death nature of medical treatment makes it all the more urgent that the government allow the marketplace to function rationally.

Restoring the marketplace requires aggressive free-market reforms. This means adjusting the tax law to end the subsidy for expensive comprehensive insurance. Moreover, Medicare should be privatized. One possibility would be to maintain the program for the current elderly, offer a phase-out option utilizing medical savings accounts (akin to IRAs) for the middle-aged, and inform young people that they will be responsible for saving for old-age medical care.

SOCIALIST PRINCIPLES REMAIN

The problem is not just getting people to understand economics, however. Despite the collapse of communism throughout the world, and the failure of welfare-state democracies in Western Europe, American politicians of all stripes still insist that more government control over health care is needed.

How can this be? In a recent Canadian survey, the majority of respondents stated that their socialized system, for all its problems, reflected their collective "generosity and compassion," and gave them at least one clear claim to being "morally superior" to the United States. Imagine! A socialist system that provides—indeed, even mandates—pain, suffering, inefficiency, and stagnation is considered to be morally superior to a capitalistic system which (when allowed to function without interference) promotes competition, technological superiority, affordability, and individual respect. In other words, it is better for everyone to have mediocre (or worse) medical care, as is the case in Canada, than it is for there to be any variation in care. Unfortunately, Americans, too, are increasingly choosing this same ethical perspective.

THE "RIGHT" TO HEALTH CARE

This attitude is reflected in the belief that health care is a "right." Dr. Ted Rumble, an orthopedic surgeon in Toronto who is cooperating with the doctors' protest movement in Canada, summed up the issue: "The public doesn't want a high quality medical system, it wants a free system." My own experience suggests that Rumble's statement applies as much to the United States as to Canada. Many people resent the fact that they cannot have something for nothing, particularly medical care. In a way, who can blame them? Government health policies already make nearly everyone dependent on a third party. So many American adults feel that their medical care should just be available—somehow—as if health care grew on trees.

The result is a refusal to deal with reality. The mere fact that health care, or whatever else, for that matter, does not grow on trees is irrelevant. "There ought to be a law" to make the desired good or service grow on trees. Of course, politicians are always delighted to participate in the charade, if it means advancing their short-term interests.

WAITING LISTS FOR SPECIALIST CARE	
Median wait, in weeks, for specialist care in Canada	
Ophthalmology	24.6
Orthopedic	20.7
Cardiovascular (bypass)	18.2
Neurosurgery	16.5
Otolaryngology	12.2
Gynecology	11.6
Internal Medicine	7.8
General Surgery	7.1

Data: Fraser Institute, 1997.

This is evident in Canada, where frustrated citizens don't want to replace the socialized system with a free market, but rather, to increase government's power to limit "unnecessary" medical visits. In a word: rationing. The childish attachment to the idea of government medicine, in Canada and elsewhere, appears at times almost mystical. A *New York Times* reporter has described the "sacred place in the shrine of Canadian values" its citizens seem to hold for its disastrous medical system. Similar sentiments are obvious in Great Britain, where former Prime Minister Margaret Thatcher could implement no real reforms in the socialized medical system, despite its obvious failures.

Incredibly, the Canadian survey actually found people divided over whether doctors should tell patients that their treatment may not be the best available. (A similar debate is currently underway in the United States over whether HMO doctors should tell their patients when they are being denied superior treatment.) A significant number said they would have more peace of mind simply not knowing. Psychologists call this "denial."

DOCTORS FIGHT BACK: MEDICINE'S LAST CHANCE

In the midst of the Canadian health-care crisis (and the growing American one) there exists one hopeful development: the protest of Canadian doctors against the socialized system. More and more doctors are refusing to accept new referrals. They are pressuring the government to reduce what it takes from them for alleged "administrative costs." They have also fought the government's attempt to force urban Toronto doctors out of their practices into more rural areas farther north. Some 700 doctors fled Canada for the United States in 1996, more than twice the number who emigrated ten years ago. If Canadian physicians can find the courage to fight irrational and unjust government mandates, then perhaps American doctors—who still enjoy more freedom than their Canadian counterparts—can muster the same courage.

Doctors must not be afraid to point out that capitalism delivers the goods. Because it respects the rights of the individual, it is the only proper, humane, and moral social system. Moreover, great medical care would never have been possible in a society that did not respect the rights of doctors. When told about a patient's refusal to pay for his services, Dr. Aaron Shutt, a fictitious surgeon in the CBS television series "Chicago Hope," stated: "It's not about money. It is about respect. Surgery is my art. It's my craft. It's mine to sell; it's mine to give away. People . . . think it's free for the taking. Well, it's not. And I'm going to do something about it."

It's time for all doctors to do something about it.

> "[Medical savings accounts] can
> bring 50 percent or more of all U.S.
> outlays for health care under the
> sway of market forces."

MEDICAL SAVINGS ACCOUNTS WILL IMPROVE THE HEALTH CARE SYSTEM

Peter J. Ferrara

In the following viewpoint, Peter J. Ferrara, chief economist at the lobbying group Americans for Tax Reform, argues that medical savings accounts (MSAs) are a superior alternative to traditional health insurance. Instead of comprehensive health insurance, under MSAs employees purchase less expensive catastrophic health insurance, which only covers expenses that exceed a higher deductible of about $3,000 per year. The savings are put into individual savings accounts, and workers pay for routine health care with money from these accounts. By allowing people to pay for health services directly rather than through an insurer, Ferrara believes MSAs encourage patients to make more cost-conscious decisions, enable them to choose the doctors and hospitals they prefer, and foster price competition within the health care industry.

As you read, consider the following questions:

1. What may an employee do at the end of each year with the unused money in his account, according to the author?
2. In Ferrara's view, what are the maximum out-of-pocket expenses under a typical MSA as compared to standard insurance plans?
3. What percent of workers who are offered the option choose medical savings accounts, according to Ferrara?

Reprinted from Peter J. Ferrara, "A New Prescription," The Wilson Quarterly, Summer 1996, by permission of the author.

Years of debate have not produced much agreement on the future of the American health-care system. But people who study the system are virtually unanimous in their diagnosis of what's wrong with the country's traditional forms of health-care financing. The patient (with advice from a doctor) ultimately decides what services and care are purchased, but another party—an insurance company, or the government, through Medicaid or Medicare—pays the bills.

THE FUNDAMENTAL FLAW

As a matter of basic economics, this is a prescription for runaway health costs. In deciding what to purchase, patients have no incentive to weigh costs against benefits, for the simple reason that someone else is paying the bill. As a result, they are likely to buy any service that offers any conceivable benefit regardless of cost—from a test of dubious utility to perhaps a minor surgical procedure. And consumers' lack of concern has ripple effects. When patients are not careful shoppers, doctors and hospitals do not adequately compete to control costs. They compete instead primarily on the basis of quality.

This fundamental flaw can be overcome only by uniting in one party the ultimate power to decide what services are purchased and the responsibility to pay for those services. There are only two ways this can be done. One is to shift the ultimate power to decide from the patient to the third-party payer. This is what is done in government-financed health-care systems: through rationing, the government or some deputized third party ultimately decides what health-care patients receive. This is also the approach taken by health maintenance organizations and other managed-care plans. The insurer ultimately decides what care patients will receive. This was the essence of President Bill Clinton's ill-fated health-care plan. It is also the reason why the proposal was so soundly defeated. The American people simply do not want to surrender control over their own health-care decisions to a third party. And who can blame them?

PROVIDING AN INCENTIVE TO CONTROL COSTS

The only other way to overcome the defect of traditional health-care financing is to turn the purse strings over to the patient. This is the idea behind medical savings accounts (MSAs). In a traditional system, employers and employees buy all health coverage from an insurer. With MSAs, the insurer is paid a much more modest sum for catastrophic insurance, which covers only bills over a high deductible of perhaps $3,000 per year. The rest of the money that would have gone to the insurance company is paid instead into an individual account for each worker. He can then use the funds to pay his medical bills below the deductible amount, choosing any medical services or treatments he wants. If there is money left in the account at the end of the year, he can, depending on how the system is designed, roll it over or withdraw it and use it for any purpose he pleases.

Workers with MSAs, therefore, spend what is in effect their own money for noncatastrophic health care. As a result, they have every incentive to control costs. They will seek to avoid unnecessary care or tests, look for doctors and hospitals that will provide quality care at the best prices, and consider whether each proffered service is worth the cost. If MSAs were in wide use, they would stimulate true cost competition among doctors and hospitals, who would seek not only to maximize quality, as they do now, but to minimize costs as well.

MSAs already exist and, despite a substantial tax disadvantage compared with standard health insurance, they are rapidly growing in popularity. Under current law, the dollars that employees pay toward health insurance are excluded from taxable income, but MSA contributions are not. (Legislation according MSAs equal treatment is under consideration in Congress.) Nevertheless, more than 3,000 employers in the United States now offer MSAs to their employees, including Forbes magazine and Dominion Resources, a Virginia utility company. The United Mine Workers union has negotiated a plan for about 15,000 employees of coal mine operators. Perhaps the leading example of MSAs in practice is at Golden Rule Insurance Company, which has offered the plan to its 1,300 workers in Indianapolis. In 1994, more than 90 percent of the company's workers chose MSAs, and they received an average year-end rebate of about $1,000, half the amount deposited in the account. Yet health costs for the company dropped about 30 percent from what they would have been with traditional health insurance.

THE BENEFITS OF MSAS

Typically, an MSA plan might have a $3,000 deductible and $2,000 or more per year in the savings account, leaving maximum out-of-pocket exposure for the worker of $1,000 per year. By contrast, under a standard traditional insurance plan with a $500 deductible and a 20 percent copayment fee on the next $3,000, out-of-pocket expenses could reach $1,500 per year. The MSAs also offer, in effect, "first-dollar" coverage: the first $2,000 in expenses can be paid directly out of the account, with no deductible.

Critics charge that if MSAs were more widely available, only the healthy would choose them, leaving the sick "ghettoized" in increasingly expensive conventional plans. But it is easy to see why this is wrong. With less out-of-pocket exposure, and with first-dollar coverage as well as complete freedom to spend the money as they see fit, the sick as well as the healthy would prefer MSAs. This has been the experience with the firms that already offer the option. More than 90 percent of workers who are given a choice pick MSAs, with no differences between the healthy and the sick. Moreover, workers who become sick show no tendency to leave MSAs.

In practice, MSAs have also increased the use of cost-effective preventive care. That is because of their first-dollar coverage for any care the patient chooses, including preventive care. Many traditional plans, by contrast, do not cover the costs of routine checkups and other preventive care. At Golden Rule, about 20 percent of the company's workers reported in a survey that they used funds in their accounts to pay for preventive care they would not have bought under the company's traditional insurance policy. What the MSA patient *does* have is an incentive to avoid preventive care that costs more than it yields in benefits. Good candidates for trimming, for example, are the batteries of tests that often get ordered up. (John Goodman, president of the National Center for Policy Analysis, has pointed out that we could spend the entire gross national product on prevention simply by getting every American to take all of the blood tests that are currently available.)

NOT A PANACEA

It is true, as critics argue, that when people exhaust their MSAs and begin to draw on their catastrophic coverage, we revert to the problematic arrangement of traditional health care: the patient is choosing services but an insurer is paying the bill. But the potential savings from MSAs are so vast that this problem should not be our first concern. If they are designed with reasonable deductibles, MSAs can bring 50 percent or more of all U.S. outlays for health care under the sway of market forces. Overall, they have the potential to cut our $1 trillion national health-care bill by 30 percent or more.

Vast savings are not the only benefit. Instead of granting even more power to government, big insurance companies, and managed-care bureaucracies, MSAs would shift control of health care to individual workers and patients, and to the doctors and hospitals they choose to serve them. In short, they would solve the health cost problem by giving more power to the people.

| "Medical savings accounts are a poison for the health care system."

MEDICAL SAVINGS ACCOUNTS WILL NOT IMPROVE THE HEALTH CARE SYSTEM

Part I: Jonathan Cohn, Part II: Edward Kennedy

In the first part of the following two-part viewpoint, Jonathan Cohn, executive editor of the *New Republic*, argues that although medical savings accounts are a sincere effort to foster consumer choice in the health care market, they will do little to improve the health care system. Cohn contends that only healthy people would be attracted to MSAs. In the second part of this viewpoint, Senator Edward Kennedy, a democrat from Massachusetts, argues that MSAs will severely harm the health care system. He believes that MSAs give a tax break to the healthy and the wealthy at the expense of the sick, and that people with MSAs will be less likely to seek preventive health care.

As you read, consider the following questions:

1. In Cohn's view, why are MSAs a good deal for the healthy?
2. In Cohn's opinion, what problem with the health care market have conservatives failed to recognize?
3. How does the American Academy of Actuaries describe MSAs, as quoted by Kennedy?

Part I: Reprinted from Jonathan Cohn, "Cosmetic Surgery: The Cheap Thrill of HMO Bashing," *The New Republic*, August 17, 1998, by permission of *The New Republic*. Copyright ©1998 The New Republic, Inc. Part II: Reprinted from Edward Kennedy, "Medical Savings Accounts Are Welfare for the Rich," syndicated column, May 12, 1996, by permission of Scripps Howard News Service.

I

Conservatives understand and confront one basic truth about health care: it is an imperfect market. In a normal market system, the purchaser of a product is the one who uses it—if you want a car, you buy yourself a car, and you weigh the trade-offs between cost and quality. You may want a Corvette, but you don't think it's worth an extra $20,000; so you buy a Toyota instead. In health care, of course, the party that buys health care is not usually the party that receives it. The majority of Americans receive health insurance through their employers; their employers, in turn, negotiate with one or several plans over cost.

AN IMPERFECT MARKET

Hypothetically, employers are supposed to consider the interests of their employees when they strike these bargains. But, as you might expect, the employers are usually most concerned with premiums. So the market system breaks down. Even when people want better insurance, they often have little or no ability to get it. Thus, the conservatives say, the answer to our health care problem is to break the link between employment and health care—that is, to give consumers the direct power to purchase their own insurance.

This certainly sounds like a good idea. The yoking together of jobs and health insurance, after all, is a historical accident. In World War II, wage controls prohibited employers from enticing workers with higher salaries, so they offered health care as a fringe benefit instead. We've been stuck with the system ever since. Government could break this link by creating purchasing pools, allowing small firms and individuals to band together, thus offering their employees more options from which to choose; by changing the tax treatment of health insurance, so that it's not prohibitively expensive for individuals and the self-employed; and by encouraging the use of individual savings accounts (known as medical savings accounts, or MSAs) that make individuals bear more of the costs of their own health care. All three ideas are in the bill the Republican House passed on July 24, 1998. Steve Forbes has indicated that he will make MSAs a cornerstone of his likely presidential campaign.

AN OVERWHELMING FLAW

Unfortunately, while the instinct to empower consumers and expand choice is a healthy one, the conservative version of this idea has an overwhelming flaw—a flaw that becomes most apparent when you consider the probable impact of MSAs. An MSA is a special savings account into which you and your employer deposit money. If you get sick, you pay for your health care bills by withdrawing from the account, up to a certain limit, at which point your insurance kicks in. (When you start an MSA, you're generally required to take out a catastrophic insurance policy, which covers you in case of a really expensive ailment.) What you don't spend you keep.

Now, is an MSA a good bargain for you? Well, if you're young and healthy, it's a great deal. After all, you're probably not going to spend that MSA money, so you'll be that much richer. But, if you're not young or you're not healthy, you're probably going to opt for a more traditional insurance plan. You can see where this is going. If MSAs were widespread, you'd have a bifurcated insurance market: Healthy people would have MSAs, and sick people would have insurance. And, of course, since the pool of people in the traditional plans would then be sicker on average, the plans would have to charge higher premiums to cover the costs. A lot of these people would lose coverage, and even those who didn't would end up with all the quality problems people now face in the most restrictive managed-care plans. So you've improved quality for a few, more or less at the expense of others.

NOT AN ECONOMIC COMMODITY

The MSA problem highlights the fundamental trouble with the conservative approach to health care quality reform. Conservatives properly recognize one way in which the current health care market fails, but they miss another: deep down, for-profit insurance companies don't really want to take care of sick people. After all, sick people cost money. As long as that is the case, and as long as the entities making decisions about health care want to make profits, quality of care will continue to be a low priority. As Arnold Relman, professor emeritus at Harvard Medical School, wrote recently in The American Prospect, we need to "accept the notion of health care as a social good rather than an economic commodity."

II

Why not encourage businesses and individuals to buy less-costly high-deductible health insurance policies, and put their savings on premiums into a tax-free medical savings account that can be tapped to pay routine medical costs?

What sounds good in theory is quack medicine in practice. The current attempt to include MSAs in the Kassebaum-Kennedy health insurance reform bill risks killing the program and denying millions of Americans the help they need.

A Giveaway to the Healthy and Wealthy

Medical savings accounts are a poison for the health care system. They represent a $3 billion federal giveaway to the healthy and wealthy that will drive up insurance premiums for everyone else. They discourage preventive care. They are a handout to a handful of insurance companies that specialize in catastrophic health insurance policies that have been among the worst abusers of the present system.

MSAs give purchasers a tax incentive to buy a high-deductible health insurance policy. As passed by the House of Representatives, the annual deductible must be at least $1,500 for an individual policy and $3,000 for a family policy.

A Question of Philosophy

The MSA option will appear beneficial to younger healthier people. And that is the problem: MSAs can in effect remove the equitable distribution of risk across the whole population which is the underpinnings of traditional insurance. This is why an MSA program cannot exist side-by-side with a national health program like Medicare or a Canadian-style single-payer system.

So what's wrong with scrapping Medicare and plans for other national systems altogether in favor of a full-blown MSA program, you might ask.

Ultimately, the issue comes down to a question of philosophy. MSAs treat health care as nothing more than a market commodity and asks that consumers examine their health coverage the same way they do their auto insurance. They demand that patients exercise great discipline in maintaining their accounts. Make one mistake, empty your MSA, and you're in big trouble.

In my view, health care is something more than a service or a product. It often is the difference between life and death and it should be treated like a right, not a privilege for the financially savvy.

Such policies are most attractive to the healthy. They like the lower premiums and the tax break, and are willing to gamble on their health. As healthy individuals and families choose MSAs, the cost of insurance for everyone else goes up—an increase in premiums of 60 percent or even much higher, according to the Urban Institute.

The nonpartisan Congressional Budget Office says that medical savings accounts "could threaten the existence of standard health insurance." The prestigious American Academy of Actuaries calls MSAs a tax on the sick to benefit the healthy.

Because the tax benefits of medical savings accounts are most attractive to those in high-income tax brackets who can afford to pay the higher deductibles, they result in all taxpayers subsidizing the well-off. The Congressional Joint Tax Committee estimates that only 1 percent of the tax benefits would go to people with incomes of less than $30,000 a year.

DISCOURAGING PREVENTIVE CARE

High-deductible policies also discourage timely preventive care—because insurance coverage begins only after $1,500 or $3,000 has already been paid out. A bias against preventive care means higher health costs for all in the long run.

The driving force behind MSAs is the Golden Rule Insurance Co. of Indianapolis, Ind., which has made $1.5 million in political contributions, including major contributions to powerful members of the House and Senate. The company has a history of canceled policies, large premium increases for the sick, and fine print that excludes whole body parts from coverage. Such coverage could literally cost you an arm and a leg.

The Kassebaum-Kennedy health insurance reform bill is consensus legislation—it passed the Senate by a rare 100-0 vote. It guarantees every individual and family that, as long as they faithfully pay their premiums, they cannot be denied health insurance coverage, even if they change jobs, lose their jobs or become seriously ill.

It also protects people in these situations against new exclusions for pre-existing conditions. Medical savings accounts would fracture this consensus and deny this long overdue help to the 25 million Americans who would benefit from these changes.

[The Kassebaum-Kennedy Bill, also known as the Health Insurance Portability Act, became law in 1996. It included a measure that allows 750,000 tax-free MSAs to be sold on a four-year experimental basis.]

"[Single-payer national health insurance] offers the most promising way to achieve universal access while keeping costs reasonably under control."

THE UNITED STATES SHOULD ADOPT NATIONAL HEALTH INSURANCE

David DeGrazia

In the following viewpoint, David DeGrazia argues that a single payer system of national health insurance is the best way to provide health coverage to all Americans. Under a single payer system, the government pays for all health care expenses (in contrast to the U.S. system, in which the government, individuals, employers, and private insurers each pay a portion of health care bills). He contends that there is widespread support for universal access to health care among Americans, but that antigovernment sentiment and lobbying by special interest groups have prevented national health insurance from receiving a fair hearing in American politics. DeGrazia is a professor of philosophy at George Washington University in Washington, D.C.

As you read, consider the following questions:

1. According to DeGrazia, what are the only two industrialized nations that do not provide universal access to health care?
2. How many cents of each health care dollar does the author say are spent on administration in the United States and in Canada, respectively?
3. In DeGrazia's view, what types of special interest groups have lobbied to oppose serious health care reform?

Reprinted, with permission, from David DeGrazia, "Why the United States Should Adopt a Single Payer System of Health Care Finance," *Kennedy Institute of Ethics Journal*, June 1996, pp. 145–56; ©1996 The Johns Hopkins University Press.

The American health care system is deeply troubled, and nothing short of radical restructuring will come close to solving its major problems. Congressional proposals to cut Medicare and to partially dismantle Medicaid would, at best, slightly slow the skyrocketing health expenditures, while increasing burdens on the elderly and guaranteeing that fewer indigent will have access to needed care. These proposals to change the two largest American public health care programs appeared approximately one year after the Clinton reform plan was laid to rest. The most recent serious discussions of systemic health care reform, including an impressive array of legislative proposals, were buried at the same political funeral.

REFORM IS STILL NEEDED

Although nothing could be less fashionable today than talk of comprehensive health care reform, the major problems of American health care have not gone away. The United States and South Africa are the only remaining industrialized nations that fail to provide universal access to health care. Approximately 40 million Americans lack any form of health insurance at a given time. Some 59 million Americans go without health insurance for part of the year. This failure of access occurs despite the highest per capita spending on health care in the world: 14 to 15 percent of the gross national product, with costs rising at an average of 11.5 percent per year. In some respects, the high-technology capabilities for which American medicine is renowned actually frustrate the nation's medical goals. This is due not only to the extraordinary costs of such technology, but also to their proliferation and duplication in an unconstrained (non)system, as Gordon D. Schiff et al. point out in a 1994 *Journal of the American Medical Association* article:

> For example, because we have too many mammography machines, each is underutilized. This doubles the cost of each test. As a result, many women cannot afford screening. Thus, because we have too many mammography machines, we have too little breast cancer screening.

Nor does American health care sail smoothly for insured patients and those who serve them. Underinsurance is a major problem. The policies that cover millions of Americans would not cover the costs of a major illness; such costs are a leading reason for bankruptcy today. Many people are afraid to change jobs for fear of losing their insurance. Rising insurance costs generally either slow wage increases or get passed on to workers in the form of higher premiums. Medicare patients are sometimes avoided by health care providers seeking higher payment from patients with private insurance. The problem is worse for Medicaid patients, who frequently receive substandard care. Exploding health expenditures have led to cost containment efforts that add to the administrative hassles physicians must endure and that, ironically, tend to increase overall spending through the inefficiencies of micromanagement. Physicians David U. Himmelstein and Steffie Woolhandler write that:

> In private practice, we waste countless hours on billing and bureaucracy. . . . Diagnosis-related groups (DRGs) have placed us between administrators demanding early discharge and elderly patients with no one to help them at home. . . . In HMOs we walk a tightrope between thrift and penuriousness, too often under the pressure of surveillance by bureaucrats more concerned with the bottom line than with other measures of achievement.

A SINGLE-PAYER SYSTEM IS THE ANSWER

In view of these problems, the United States should adopt a single-payer system of health care finance, which offers the most promising way to achieve universal access while keeping costs reasonably under control. After briefly discussing the goals of health care reform and some common assumptions made in the debate surrounding it, I will present the case for a single-payer system (drawing mainly from the experience of Canada). In addition, I will identify several factors that prevent a fair assessment of the single-payer option in the U.S. and will argue that discussions of rationing are often vitiated by inattention to issues regarding the structure of the broader health care system.

In the 1980s and early 1990s, a vigorous philosophical discussion representing various theoretical perspectives yielded a virtual consensus that the United States has an obligation to ensure universal access to some level of health care services. Major contributors to this discussion made a common and, to my knowledge, unchallenged assumption that any massive expansion of health care coverage would entail greater overall expenditures. This assumption was reflected in animated talk about "a bottomless pit" of possible expenditures, which yawned in front of anyone so foolish as to consider universal coverage without being prepared to endorse severe restrictions on guaranteed benefits. After all, cost controls were also taken to be morally required. And surely it would be impossible to provide universal access to a comprehensive set of benefits while simultaneously keeping costs to an acceptable level! The natural conclusion was that the U.S. must strive for universal access to only a "decent minimum" of health care services.

The major goals of universal coverage and cost controls have enjoyed the support not only of many philosophical writers, but, for many years, of most of the American public as well. In this paper, I assume these two goals as a moral starting point. Anyone who does not share the goals may understand my argument in conditional form: If we assume the goals of universal coverage and cost controls, then a single-payer approach is the way to go.

DOING THE IMPOSSIBLE

According to the reasoning described in the previous section, Canada's health care system has accomplished the impossible. First, Canada provides *universal access* to care and still *controls costs* sufficiently to spend much less per capita than the U.S. does. In 1990, for example, the U.S. spent $2566 per citizen on health care while Canada—the world's second biggest spender—spent only $1770 per citizen, less than 70 percent as much. Equally surprising to many Americans, Canadians have access, not just to some "decent minimum" of health care, but to a very comprehensive set of benefits, including long-term and chronic care, as well as the services of psychiatrists and psychiatric hospitals. Commentators often state that the Canadian system provides "all medically necessary" services as determined by physicians, but the more modest claim that the health care benefits are very comprehensive is less likely to be contested. The quality of health care in Canada is generally considered high, and patient satisfaction is apparently higher than in the U.S. Equally impressive is the extensive freedom enjoyed by both providers and patients. Physicians are paid predominantly under a fee-for-service system, thereby avoiding, for example, the various kinds of restrictions imposed by American HMOs, such as limitations on the providers to whom patients can be referred and limits on the number of visits patients can make for, say, psychotherapy. In addition, Canadian physicians are undisturbed by the scrutiny and demands of insurance companies—since there are none— and they have very little administrative overhead, as explained below. At the same time, patients enjoy the freedom to choose their physicians (something many Americans cannot do); the freedom to receive appropriate medical care regardless of wealth, employment status, or preexisting conditions; and the freedom from fear that such coverage allows. Patients also are free of copayments, deductibles, and the like, since, with rare exceptions, such as Quebec's $2 user fee for its drug plan subscribers, they are not charged for medical services. How are the achievements of Canada's health care system possible?

Canada Eliminates Administrative Waste

Canada is able to get more for less chiefly because of (1) the vastly reduced administrative expenses made possible by the absence of a private insurance industry (competing payers) and (2) the economic controls afforded by global budgeting. While the U.S. spends an estimated 25 cents of every health care dollar on administration, Canada spends on the order of 13 cents. The U.S. has more than 1,500 different payers. Most of them, as part of the private sector, must advertise, elaborate their unique restrictions on coverage, determine patient eligibility, conduct patient-by-patient utilization reviews, bill patients individually, try to collect on bad debts, and the like—all while still seeking a profit. *Nearly all of this frenetic activity is eliminated in Canada.* Physicians submit simple, standardized forms—or disks—on which they check off the services rendered; they are then reimbursed by provincial governments.

Global budgeting and other planning is also crucial in controlling costs. Canada pays physicians on the basis of standardized fees negotiated annually by medical and government representatives. Also negotiated annually are the global budgets for hospitals, which cover all expenses and therefore virtually eliminate the need to bill patients. In addition, Canada limits the number of specialty physicians, allocates the purchase of costly equipment, and restricts expensive procedures such as open-heart surgery to a few hospitals in major population centers.

Apparently, such macromanagement is far more cost-effective than the highly intensive micromanagement of the American system, with its myriad insurance companies scrutinizing decisions, patient eligibility, and so on, thereby creating mountains of paperwork for whole armies of administrators to climb. This claim of cost-effectiveness is supported by the fact that the systems of other industrial countries, including the single payers of the Scandinavian countries, France, Great Britain, and others, which have favored macromanagement, have had lower rates of health care inflation in recent decades than the U.S. has had. Not only does the U.S. currently spend more per capita than other countries, but the gap keeps growing.

These differences in the financing of American and Canadian health care make sense of the claim by the editor of *The New England Journal of Medicine* that "we are now spending so much on health care that we could cover all medically indicated care for all Americans without any additional spending." Indeed, of the many plans submitted to Congress in the flurry of activity preceding the Clinton plan's demise, the Congressional Budget Office (CBO) found a single-payer approach to be the only one likely to provide universal coverage while saving money, an estimated 14 billion dollars annually. An earlier study by the General Accounting Office (GAO), which was based on less optimistic assumptions, estimated that an American single-payer system would save about 3 billion dollars annually while achieving universal coverage. . . .

Obstacles to Giving the Single-Payer System a Fair Hearing

The Canadian single-payer system boasts universal access to a very comprehensive set of benefits, the availability of high-quality care, and extensive—although not unlimited—freedom for both patients and providers. At the same time, it spends considerably less per capita than the American system. Despite the relative success of the Canadian system, however, the single-payer approach has yet to receive a fair hearing in the U.S. for several reasons.

First, wealthy special-interest groups with a financial stake in maintaining something resembling the status quo have exerted herculean political muscle in recent discussions of health care reform. Such groups include the Health Insurance Association of America, which produced the influential Harry and Louise television ads designed to undermine the Clinton reform efforts; the pharmaceutical industry; and various physician groups, including the American Medical Association. Although Americans who support serious reform vastly outnumber those represented by these lobbies, the former are relatively unorganized. Charles Lewis, writing in the *Washington Post*, describes what such Americans are up against:

> In 1993 and 1994, hundreds of special interests cumulatively have spent in excess of $100 million to influence the outcome of this public policy issue. According to [various] sources, at least 97 firms have been hired . . . to influence this debate. Those firms and other health care clients have hired at least 80 former congressional and executive branch officials; of that total, 23 former officials, including 12 former members of Congress, left the government in 1993 or 1994 to work for health care interests.

It is almost axiomatic that wealthier lobbies—who largely oppose serious reform—are more influential than lobbies of modest means. In addition, I doubt that anyone who has followed the reform debate closely will object to my assertion that the political repertoire of lobbies opposing reform includes fear mongering and misinformation.

FAITH IN THE FREE MARKET

A second reason that it is difficult for the single payer to get a fair hearing in the U.S. is America's (almost religious) faith in the efficiency of the free market. Specifically, it often is simply assumed that a mixed financing system that includes insurance companies—a free-market component—as well as public programs will be more efficient than a single payer, thanks to competition among payers in the mixed system. (Almost no one seems to favor the complete abolition of public programs.) . . .

There are several reasons why competition in health care may fail to increase efficiency. First, "consumers" of health care are relatively uninformed about medical options—in contrast to car or stereo buyers, who on the whole know enough about these goods to get value for their money. Moreover, the Harry and Louise ads and other phenomena of the recent health care debate remind us that misinforming or misleading consumers can be big business in health care. Second, although classical economics makes the idealizing assumption that consumers' choices are voluntary, many patients' choices are substantially nonvoluntary due to the compromising effects of illness, fear, suffering, and (quite often) lack of insurance. Indeed, many medical decisions are not made by patients or their surrogates at all; emergency rooms offer familiar examples. There are other reasons why competition in health care may fail to increase efficiency, but exploring these factors would take us deeper into economic theory than is possible here.

THE ASSUMPTION OF INCREASED BUREAUCRACY

A third obstacle to the single payer's receiving a fair hearing is the common assumption that more government involvement means more bureaucracy. Since federal and state governments would be the sole payers in such a system, the American mind tends to imagine new legions of government bureaucrats dragging down the system with red tape and inefficiency. This apprehension seems especially likely today when antigovernment sentiment is as high as it is. But an evaluation of reform options must provide a comparison of the bureaucracy of the present system, the bureaucracy that would exist in alternative systems, and the bureaucracy entailed by a single payer. Americans tend to forget about the administrative expenses of *competing insurance companies* and tend to assume, I think, that the private sector is relatively streamlined whereas the public sector is the opposite. But, in large part, it is precisely the massive reduction of administration in a single-payer system that permits it to spend less per capita than the current U.S. system, while achieving so many health care goals.

What Is a Universal Health Care System?

A universal health care system simply means that everyone's health care is paid for out of a common national fund. A universal, not-for-profit, single payer national health insurance system thus replaces our current profit-driven, multi-payer system that leaves 42 million people uninsured, and insured patients at risk of being denied care when they are sick so corporations can profit.

Every resident has a national health care card which they can use for care at any hospital, clinic, doctor's office, or other medical facility in the country regardless of age, income, or employment. Funding is collected through a sliding scale of income and payroll taxes and placed in a national health care trust fund. Publicly accountable health boards in each state administer the funds and negotiate fees and budgets with health professionals, not-for-profit HMOs, hospitals, and drug companies (taking care to minimize incentives for both undercare and overcare).

National health insurance is absolutely necessary if we are to remedy the problems in the health care system that have so long plagued nurses and their patients. It will save over $100 billion annually by reducing the amount of money spent on overhead and profits (over 25% of every health care dollar). This money can be devoted to care-givers and their patients. . . .

For-profit insurers/HMOs, hospitals, and other powerful interests do not believe that health care should be a right. These special interests are why most Americans don't know that we can afford coverage for all without sacrificing quality patient care.

Nurses' Network for a National Health Program website,
http://ideanurse.com/nnnhp.

Of course, some have characterized the Canadian system as "socialized" medicine, a charge that opens few minds in the U.S. It may be worth noting that public education, Social Security, national defense, the National Institutes of Health, and military medicine in the U.S. are all socialized (yet few critics wish their disappearance). These programs are government-financed and providers of the services work for the government. In contrast, the single-payer system in Canada (and as proposed here) is government-financed but the providers work privately. To the extent that their situation allows, patients choose their doctors on the basis of satisfaction—entailing competition among providers—but not price, since fees are standardized.

THE ASSUMPTION OF POLITICAL INFEASIBILITY

A fourth and final impediment to a fair hearing for the single-payer system is the quick assumption of political infeasibility. . . . The Clintons made a judgment early in their plans for health care reform that a single-payer system, despite its many advantages, was politically infeasible, so they opted for managed competition.

There is no question that only considerable courage in a president and many members of Congress could counter the political muscle of the special-interest groups discussed above. But it might just be possible to sell the American public on the idea of . . . universal coverage. . . . We must not assume that the slaying of recent health care reform proposals reflects the values of the broader public. To understate the point, sometimes lobbies are able to influence legislators more than the public at large can. I conclude, then, that it is not yet clear whether a single-payer approach is politically feasible in the United States. *After all, it has yet to receive a fair hearing.* On the other hand, if American politics make it *impossible* for a single-payer approach to get a reasonably fair hearing in the U.S., which I doubt, then the approach might indeed be politically infeasible. . . .

RADICAL CHANGE IS NEEDED

This paper began with the contention that the U.S. health care system is in terrible shape and that, given the lack of serious discussion of reform since the Clinton plan was buried, there is no reason to expect significant improvement in the major areas of concern. Some commentators speak cheerfully about the promise of managed care, as exemplified in HMOs and Preferred Provider Organizations. But absent a major restructuring of the broader health care system, the managed care movement promises at best a modest slowing of health care inflation, while further restricting the freedom of patients and providers and leaving untouched the national disgrace of 40 million uninsured people.

Nothing short of a radical change in the way the U.S. finances health care—specifically, a single-payer system—will allow the achievement of universal coverage while keeping costs reasonably under control and meeting other important goals.

"If Congress just let the rest of us in on its health-care deal [FEHBP], insurance would no longer be a problem for the great majority of Americans."

THE FEDERAL EMPLOYEE HEALTH BENEFITS PROGRAM IS A MODEL FOR HEALTH CARE REFORM

Eric B. Schnurer

In the following viewpoint, Eric B. Schnurer argues that the Federal Employee Health Benefits Program (FEHBP) should be made available to all Americans. FEHBP is a government program but is made up of hundreds of private health plans, each competing to serve a portion of FEHBP's 10 million enrollees. Schnurer believes that this framework combines the safeguards of government—the elderly and other high-risk individuals cannot be excluded from the program—with the benefits of private competition. Health plans participating in FEHBP cost much less than those that do not, according to the author. Schnurer is president of Public Works, a public policy analysis and consulting firm.

As you read, consider the following questions:

1. How many health plans does the author say participate in FEHBP?
2. What argument did opponents use to block Senator George Mitchell's proposed expansion of FEHBP in 1994, according to the author?
3. In Schnurer's opinion, how would opening FEHBP up to all Americans benefit even those people who choose not to join the plan?

Reprinted, with permission, from Eric B. Schnurer, "Health Care Plan Most of Us Could Buy," The Washington Monthly, April 1998. Copyright by The Washington Monthly Company, 1611 Connecticut Ave. NW, Washington, DC 20009; (202) 462-0128.

Ruth Kain didn't exactly get the best deal possible. Kain lives in the little town of Ava, Mo., where she and her husband of 47 years, Rufus, settled after he retired in 1990. Rufus had been able to retain his company health insurance until he qualified for Medicare, at which point Ruth was allowed by Rufus' former employer to buy a COBRA plan for 36 months. When that expired, Ruth was 63 and not yet eligible for Medicare; nor, as a result of a heart ailment constituting a "pre-existing condition," could she find a private insurer willing to cover her in the interim.

Ruth Kain is just the type of person legislators were trying to help when they passed the 1996 Kennedy-Kassebaum bill requiring insurance companies to provide coverage even to Americans with pre-existing medical conditions. Alas, private carriers have hardly been leaping to assume this new responsibility. (I know: You are shocked—*shocked*—to hear that health insurers wouldn't insure people who need health care.) Many penalize agents who write such policies, while one—exploiting a loophole in the law that says insurers need not provide coverage for a condition that has gone uninsured for the last 63 days—actually stretches out the processing of applications from individuals with pre-existing conditions for more than 63 days, and then routinely denies the request. When they do make coverage available, it is often at rates double the norm.

A Bum Deal

The end result: Even with Kennedy-Kassebaum in place, Kain couldn't obtain insurance that would cover her heart problems. And sure enough, as all such stories go, after shelling out $10,000 for a pacemaker that her policy didn't cover, she began experiencing severe chest pains in November 1997 and wound up spending Thanksgiving in the hospital. To cover the bill for her stay—a daunting $14,000—she and Rufus were forced to sell the farm they lived on.

Clearly, Ruth Kain had gotten a bum deal.

President Clinton seemed to agree. In January 1998, he proposed an expansion of Medicare, the federal health insurance program for the elderly, to cover people like Kain. Under the Clinton plan, retirees from age 62 to 65, as well as people over age 55 who have been laid off and lost insurance, could buy into Medicare for more or less the actual price of such coverage. (Those in the early retiree group would pay slightly lower premiums than other new entrants, but would make up for it with slightly higher monthly payments once admitted to "regular" Medicare at 65.) This is a pretty good deal, cheaper-by-half than the $1,000-a-month that Kain could expect to pay a private insurer—assuming she could find one willing to issue her a policy. And so white-haired Ruth Kain from Ava, Mo., stood by Bill Clinton in the White House as the president unveiled his grand plan.

Republicans, with their usual flair, promptly declared the president's proposal Dead On Arrival. First they wheeled out the standard objection to Medicare expansion: With the impending retirement of the massive Baby Boom generation, the system is already too financially shaky to pile even more beneficiaries onto the program. ("If you're on the Titanic, you wouldn't invite more people to join you," huffed one GOP congressman.) But Clinton basically rendered this argument moot by proposing that recipients essentially pay their own way.

ADVERSE SELECTION

A slightly more sophisticated criticism of the plan is that it would worsen Medicare's financial problems through "adverse selection." Unlike Social Security or Medicare Part A, the president's buy-in program would be voluntary, which means a disproportionate number of the people flocking to sign up for it would be those having trouble finding alternative coverage at a reasonable price—i.e., those who present the worst health risk and thus bear the highest price-tag for coverage. This, say critics, would eventually drive Medicare's per-person costs higher, rendering it a not-so-good deal for those already in it.

Finally, Republicans fear The Slippery Slope and are aware that such a program could eventually lead to—gasp!—health insurance for all Americans, not just the old. This, of course, is the real specter haunting the right, though they have yet to articulate why wiping out the ranks of the uninsured (without using tax subsidies, mind you) is such a bad thing.

But, whatever the merits of their various concerns, on one very important point, the Republicans are right: This was still not the best deal Ruth Kain could have been offered.

We could, instead, allow Americans to buy into another existing government program, one that does not possess the problematic fiscal "pre-existing condition" that Medicare does. One in which the phenomenon of "adverse selection" is minimized. One in which the sort of consumer choice that conservatives claim they want to inject into government-run health coverage—particularly Medicare—already exists, with a vengeance. One that might actually save taxpayers money if it were expanded. One that . . . might even make sense to expand to all Americans. The program that could do all this? The Federal Employee Health Benefits Program, or FEHBP—pronounced, rather disconcertingly, as "Feeb."

THE PEOPLE'S CHOICE

With nearly 10 million enrollees nationwide, FEHBP constitutes the largest medical plan in the United States. All federal employees—as well as members of Congress, the Supreme Court, and the Cabinet—are eligible for coverage. While employees elsewhere hope for "cafeteria plans," FEHBP enrollees are treated to a virtual Valhalla of smorgasbords: A total of 380 health plans nationwide participate in FEHBP, offering the average beneficiary at least a dozen options for coverage in her locality, ranging from managed care to traditional fee-for-service. It allows enrollees to choose their own physicians. Even before Kennedy-Kassebaum, it basically insured everyone in its population, regardless of pre-existing conditions. There is no cancellation for catastrophic illness. And if the plan you choose isn't working out for you, the annual "open season" allows you easily to switch insurers within a year. Consumer satisfaction is strikingly high: 87 percent for those in fee-for-service plans and 85 percent for those in HMOs.

Most of FEHBP's features are not available to the vast majority of Americans—including beneficiaries of Medicare, where more and more seniors are simply being herded into managed care. One might therefore expect that this Cadillac of coverage plans suffers from gold-plated prices. One would be wrong. As health-care costs exploded between 1982 and 1994, FEHBP's average premium rose by approximately 3.5 percent less than did premiums for private-sector, big-business group plans. In 1994, Republican Sen. Ted Stevens (ironically, in a statement opposing extending FEHBP to non-government employees) explained: "The system holds down growth in costs by forcing insurers to compete for customers by providing the best service at the lowest premiums."

COMPETITIVE PRICING

How low? One of the largest insurers in the program, the Government Employees Health Association, offers a fee-for-service plan for single individuals at a cost of $2,548 a year ($212 per month), including both the employee's and the government's share. The full-family version prices out at $5,496 ($458 per month). The Blue Cross standard package available to FEHBP families costs $5,254 a year—about 13 percent less than the similar Blue plan offered to small groups, and $1,000 less than the average conventional plan available to the largest employers.

With this kind of competitive pricing, it's not surprising that fans ranging from Sen. Edward M. Kennedy (D-Mass.) to the Heritage Foundation have hailed FEHBP as a model for health-care reform. Republican Sen. William Roth of Delaware—co-author of the Reagan-era Kemp-Roth tax cut intended to slash government—proposed several years ago that uninsured Americans, the self-employed, and members of small groups be allowed to buy into the program. "The FEHBP is a government sponsored, private-sector operated, nationwide health care delivery system," Roth observed at the time. "It has a proven record. It could serve as an excellent vehicle for providing health care to those in our country who need it but can't afford it because they are not part of a large group." (Roth's proposal, dubbed "CareNet," would have also subsidized the purchase of coverage by the unemployed by eliminating uncompensated care reimbursements to hospitals—essentially buying the poor competitively priced insurance instead of waiting to pay for their expensive emergency room care). Senator Stevens similarly declared that FEHBP "deserves to be recognized as a basic success in health-care insurance."

MARKET POWER

Did anyone tell these guys that this is a government program?

Of course, the secret of FEHBP's success can be pinned on a fact that has nothing—and yet everything—to do with its government nature. Yes, part of FEHBP's success lies in the fact that private companies, not a government bureaucracy, design, offer, and administer the benefits; that market competition, not governmental *diktat*, determines both inputs and outcomes; and that the program is voluntary, not mandatory like Medicare and Social Security (although, with the government paying a large share of the premiums, an eligible individual would have to be nuts not to enroll). But the main reason the Federal Employee Health Benefits Program can cut such good deals with insurers rests on the most basic of capitalist concepts: Market Power. When it comes to access to health-insurance consumers, FEHBP is the 10-million-pound gorilla. The brass ring. The Holy Grail. With 10 million people looking to spend about $1,000 apiece each year—$10 billion!—on your product, what insurer wouldn't offer a sweet deal in order to get a piece of the action? In essence, it's the same sort of advantage that entrepreneurs like John D. Rockefeller have understood and pressed since the time of Croesus. Only here's the catch: The predator exploiting its oligopsony (that's the demand-side version of "oligopoly") power is the government. So far, even Bill Gates hasn't been able to put together the purchasing clout of the federal government. And therein lies not just the path to more affordable, more consumer-friendly health coverage for more Americans, but a template for the role of government in the future—a future in which there will be more competition and government will be less powerful, less like government as we've known it in the Industrial Age and more like ... what? Like FEHBP!

FEHBP AS A MODEL FOR MEDICARE REFORM

The FEHBP and Medicare both are large programs run by the federal government, but the similarity ends there. The FEHBP is not experiencing the severe financial problems faced by Medicare. It is run by a very small bureaucracy that, unlike Medicare's, does not try to set prices for doctors and hospitals. It offers choices of modern benefits and private plans to federal retirees (and active workers) that are unavailable in Medicare. It provides comprehensive information to enrollees. And it uses a completely different payment system that blends a formula with negotiations to achieve a remarkable level of cost control while constantly improving benefits and enjoying wide popularity. . . .

Congress's own health plan, the FEHBP, is one of Washington's unsung success stories. For many years, it has given Members of Congress, as well as millions of active and retired federal employees, a range of modern plans and benefits unavailable to Medicare beneficiaries. And it has done so while keeping costs firmly under control. The FEHBP also includes tools for operating a choice system that could be the model for long-term reform of Medicare.

It is time to reform Medicare to make the same advantages available to America's seniors.

Stuart M. Butler and Robert E. Moffit, *Heritage Foundation Backgrounder*, June 12, 1997.

If Congress just let the rest of us in on its health-care deal, insurance would no longer be a problem for the great majority of Americans. Of course, some of the same concerns about Clinton's Medicare proposal would have to be addressed. Which brings us back to the issue of adverse selection. As with the Medicare expansion idea, the people who would find the chance to buy into FEHBP most appealing are those who arguably present the greatest risk of high health-care costs: small business owners and employees, other non-group members, and those who are legally entitled to coverage under Kennedy-Kassebaum but can't afford it. But this will prove less of a problem than it first appears—and certainly less than with the Clinton plan.

First, we need to separate the "high risk" group into two categories: statistical and actual. Small businesses and their workers currently pay more for insurance than do large groups—not because they have higher health-care costs, but because they pose higher statistical risks. Think of it like this: Could you better predict the likely outcome of one coin flip or of a thousand? With one flip, the odds are as good that you'll be completely wrong as that you'll be right; with a thousand, if you guess half heads and half tails, the odds are overwhelming that you'll be reasonably close. If you're at all risk-averse, or simply want to plan your finances intelligently, you'd prefer the relatively predictable outcome of a thousand tosses. This is what statisticians call "The Law of Large Numbers": the bigger the group, the smaller the risk (unless, of course, the group is selected on the basis of some risk factor, such as being residents of a leper colony). Thus, if members of a small group were suddenly made members of a large group, their "riskiness," and therefore their insurance costs, would automatically decline. In fact—and this is a crucial point—so would the riskiness and costs of the large group, because it just got even larger.

The Uninsured

Of course, the uninsured and those with pre-existing conditions, whose actual health-care costs are typically higher than average, pose a somewhat different problem. They are more like the members of the leper colony—and are treated as such in the marketplace. If these folks are allowed to buy into a program like FEHBP at the same price as the average consumer, most will jump at the chance, because it's significantly cheaper than what risk-related policies would run them. In doing so, they will drive up the cost of care for the insurance pool, resulting in either lower profit margins for the insurer or higher premiums for all other consumers. (Guess which.) This, at least, was the argument in 1994 when then-Senate Majority Leader George Mitchell (D-Maine) proposed expanding FEHBP to these groups.

In reality, however, most of the people in these categories couldn't afford to participate in a buy-in program without some sort of government subsidy like that proposed by Senator Roth under CareNet. And, strictly speaking, buy-ins aren't about subsidies. Some people might question whether this then undermines the point of health-care reform. But this begs the question. "Reform for whom?" Without doubt, it's terrible that 18 percent of non-elderly Americans have no health insurance. But 82 percent of the population has overpriced coverage. And lowering the costs of insurance overall will ultimately lead to more of the uninsured population being able to afford coverage (as well as cutting the cost to taxpayers of subsidizing coverage for the rest, should the welfare state ever make a come-back—but that's a different article). The point here is that FEHBP would be unlikely to be flooded by high-cost patients.

In any event, it turns out that FEHBP already starts with a higher-than-average-cost insurance pool: As a general rule, the older the individual, the higher the health-care costs. And while the average age of workers in the private sector is only 37.7 years, federal workers are significantly older—43.8 years, on average. What's more, 40 percent of FEHBP enrollees are retirees. So just on the basis of health spending patterns, FEHBP already is not the insurance pool ideal. Why does it achieve such good bargains then? Because of the Law of Large Numbers and the Law of the Market. And it will continue to do so even—perhaps especially—if large numbers of small-business employees and the currently uninsured choose to join. (In fact, many of the uninsured are actually young people who don't present high risks but see current insurance options as not worth the price; if they were to buy into FEHBP's over-aged pool, they would actually improve the average risk. Thus, KPMG Peat Marwick recently concluded that adding *all* the uninsured to smaller *state* government employee-risk pools "should not raise premiums considerably.")

MORE MARKET CLOUT

Moreover, if FEHBP enrollment is open to anyone, it is not just these more marginal groups who will join: Employees of any business could switch, especially if their employer continues to pay the same share of the premiums. And why wouldn't they? With wider choice, greater consumer protections, higher satisfaction, and greater market power, the federal plan is a great deal if you can get it. And the best part is: The more people who take advantage of the offer, the better a deal it becomes. Why? Because of the Law of Large Numbers and the Law of the Market.

In short, if the government became the "buying cooperative" for all of us, it could use its market clout to obtain better and better deals in the private market. This would have three effects: It would provide new and improved options for the millions of Americans looking for a better deal on their health insurance. Second, by enlarging the FEHBP pool, it would lower rates for FEHBP enrollees, meaning that the costs taxpayers are currently bearing for federal employee benefits would decrease. Third, even those Americans who chose not to buy into FEHBP would likely experience improvement in their insurance coverage. Why? Because they (or, at least, their employers) would always have the option of leaving their current plan and signing on with FEHBP if other players in the market didn't keep pace with the federal plan. The huge federal buying co-op, then, would keep constant competitive pressure on the market to lower prices and improve satisfaction for all consumers.

The government's role in this process would not be as a regulator or provider. (Recall the Republican elegy to FEHBP as a program of private-sector provided services chosen by participants through market mechanisms.) The government would act purely as a market participant, as a voluntary association of citizens, as an aggregator of consumer preferences. With government serving as a large purchasing co-operative into which any American could voluntarily buy (starting with the "critical mass" of 10 million federal employees), we would have the advantages attributed to a "single payer" system of health insurance, but without drawbacks such as inefficient government bureaucracy and involuntary participation.

Examples of government acting in such a role already exist. The Clinton administration's direct-lending program for student loans, for instance, was so successful that banks, who were losing out on the business, demanded that the "pro-competition" Republican Congress curtail it. The Postal Service's ability to compete successfully with private shippers has drawn similar opposition. God forbid that the federal government should actually offer something more efficiently than the private sector!

But the fact is that it can—aggregating the interests of millions of small economic actors, achieving economies of scale. Governments everywhere are losing the abilities to tax, regulate, and redistribute resources. Is there anything to replace them? Yes: facilitating the ability of ordinary people to act together in the marketplace in the face of larger opposing interests. Not all (or even most) market-power enhancing combinations will be "government"—but there will still be some problems that purely "private" arrangements will be unable, or unwilling, to address.

Allowing anyone to buy into FEHBP, then, may not just encourage a lower-priced, more-competitive health insurance market for all Americans. It may also mark what Bush White House adviser James Pinkerton has called "The Big Offer": a revised conception of government's role that addresses the new needs of the vast majority of people. And that could help cure more than just our health-care problems.

| "The tax code penalizes individuals who purchase insurance for themselves."

THE GOVERNMENT SHOULD ENCOURAGE INDIVIDUALLY OWNED HEALTH INSURANCE

Sue A. Blevins

In the following viewpoint, Sue A. Blevins argues that federal tax policies are responsible for many of the problems with the health care system. U.S. tax policy makes employer-provided health insurance cheaper than individually purchased health insurance; Blevins believes that this system limits people's health care choices, forcing them to pay extra taxes if they do not wish to settle for the health plan their employer offers. She says the government should implement a universal tax credit for health insurance, thus removing the financial penalty for buying health insurance individually. Blevins is president of the Institute for Health Freedom, a Washington D.C.–based think tank that advocates consumer choice in health care.

As you read, consider the following questions:

1. According to the author, what percent of Americans say that their employer offers only one health plan?
2. Why did businesses originally begin to offer health insurance to their employees, in the author's view?
3. How much more would it cost for a worker who makes $25,000 per year to buy health insurance individually rather than through his employer, according to Blevins?

Excerpted from Sue A. Blevins, "Restoring Health Freedom: The Case for a Universal Tax Credit for Health Insurance," *Cato Policy Analysis*, December 12, 1997. Reprinted by permission of the Cato Institute.

F ew issues in health care have as much resonance with the American public as the freedom to choose one's doctor or health care provider. Indeed, concern about restrictions on the free choice of provider was one of the major reasons for the defeat of the Clinton health care plan. Today, the importance of that issue can be seen in the anxiety over managed care and its restrictions.

There is good reason for Americans to be anxious. In one sense, of course, we remain free to choose any health care provider we wish—if we are willing to pay for it. However, in practice, government policies are increasingly limiting our choices.

HOW THE GOVERNMENT LIMITS CHOICE IN HEALTH CARE

The most visible of those government policies is the increasing number of state laws and federal reimbursement regulations that directly restrict patient access to the full range of available health care services, including midwives, nurse practitioners, and chiropractors. Regulations also limit consumer access to nontraditional treatments such as acupuncture, homeopathy, and massage therapy. However, a less obvious government policy may have an even greater impact on the freedom to choose the provider of one's choice. Following World War II, the federal government established a tax law that favors employer-sponsored health insurance, while penalizing individuals for purchasing private health insurance. The value of employer-provided insurance is excluded from the employee's gross income and is therefore untaxed. However, workers who purchase their own health insurance or who purchase health care out of pocket receive no tax break. They must purchase health insurance (or health care) with after-tax dollars, which dramatically increases the effective cost of the insurance or health care.

As a result of that bias in the tax code, most people have been subtly coerced into relying on third parties such as employers and governments to pay health care bills, even for routine care. Third parties paid 77 cents of every dollar spent on health care in 1990. That means that third parties decide what types of health benefits are covered for most Americans. After all, he who pays the piper calls the tune, and since employers and governments are paying the health care bills, they get to decide what is covered.

HOW TO RESTORE FREEDOM TO HEALTH CARE

Because the tax code penalizes individuals who purchase insurance for themselves, most workers rely on employer-provided insurance. As a result, however, those workers are limited in the type of insurance they receive and the type of provider that the insurance covers. In fact, 48 percent of U.S. workers report that their employers offer only one health care plan. Those plans often are health maintenance organizations (HMOs) or other types of managed care that limit the available number of physicians and treatments.

Congress has responded to this problem by attempting to mandate the type of providers and services reimbursable by health insurers. In 1996, for example, Congress mandated that insurers provide coverage for at least 48 hours of maternity care. A host of additional mandates is pending. But mandating insurance benefits is not a solution: Adding additional services drives up the cost of insurance, causes some individuals and employers to drop their insurance, and ultimately increases the number of uninsured persons.

The way to truly restore health freedom is not to treat the symptoms through mandated benefits but to cure the underlying disease by eliminating the tax bias against individually purchased health insurance. That will give individual consumers control over their health care dollars, thus restoring their freedom to choose their health care providers.

WHO REALLY PAYS FOR HEALTH INSURANCE?

Who really pays for employer-provided health insurance? Employees and taxpayers do. Most people accept limited health care choices because they think someone else—employers or government—is paying for their health insurance. But that is a misconception. As is true of every other commodity or service, there is no such thing as "free" health insurance. Employer-sponsored health insurance plans lead employees to believe they are getting free coverage, but economists show that workers actually forgo higher wages in lieu of health benefits.

Economist Charles Phelps argues that "every dollar paid for health insurance is a dollar not paid in wages. This means that workers want to be careful in their selection of insurance, because they really are paying for it, even if the employer is making the payments on paper." John Goodman, president of the National Center for Policy Analysis, puts it this way:

> Health insurance is a fringe benefit which substitutes for wages in the total employee compensation package. The more costly health insurance becomes, the smaller the remaining funds available for wage and salary increases. The ultimate victims of waste in the medical marketplace are employees. This is one reason

why take-home pay has been relatively stagnant over the past two decades, even though total compensation has been rising.

THIRD-PARTY PAYMENT DRIVES COSTS UP

... Workers also bear the burden of high health care costs by relying on third parties. When people rely on a business or other third party to pay for medical care, they consume more health care services than they would if they were paying for them directly. The following scenario demonstrates how that occurs. A group of coworkers decides to celebrate for the holiday by going out to dinner. They agree ahead of time to split the restaurant bill evenly among all workers. Paying for food collectively means that some people will order more food than they would if they were paying separately. For example, the nondrinker who doesn't normally order dessert does so because he wants to "get his money's worth," especially since the rest of the group is ordering wine. If the workers continued to dine as a group, eventually someone would complain that costs are too high. Sooner or later, there would be limits placed on the choices of foods and drinks that could be ordered.

THE CASE AGAINST EMPLOYEE BENEFITS

Company-sponsored medical insurance . . . gives employers reasons to intrude on the most personal aspects of their employees' lives, from a family's medical history to a worker's sexual orientation (in the case of domestic partner coverage). Once involved with such personal matters, it seems perfectly natural for employers to devote precious time and energy to matters of health and lifestyle, by offering smoking cessation programs, stress reduction classes, cholesterol screenings, health awareness lectures and newsletters about diet and nutrition. But whatever goodwill such nannyism might generate, it evaporates as soon as the employer increases premiums, switches managed care networks or denies a claim.

Craig J. Cantoni, *Wall Street Journal*, August 18, 1997.

Because the third-party dynamic increases spending, some economists argue that it is more efficient to purchase health care individually. For example, Eugene Steuerle, a senior fellow of the Urban Institute, stresses that individual financing of health insurance makes the cost of health care more obvious to people and leads them to demand more for their money. Steuerle notes that financing health insurance individually will increase the efficiency of the market. "In the long run, you'll get a better level of medical goods and services for less money."

Because they rely on third parties, Americans are paying higher prices for fewer choices. Today, a health insurance plan offered by a smaller business (50–199 workers) costs on average $4,848 for families and $1,932 for individuals. Annual health insurance premiums for larger employers (1,000 or more workers) run $5,400 for families and $2,067 for individuals. Those figures do not include hidden health care costs, such as federal payroll taxes for Medicare Part A, general tax revenues for Medicare Part B, and state and local taxes that support community hospitals and clinics. All told, the hidden cost of health care is well over $8,000 per household.

WHY DO AMERICANS RELY ON EMPLOYERS TO FINANCE AND MANAGE HEALTH INSURANCE?

Conventional wisdom maintains that people purchase health insurance through employers to obtain a group rate. But that is not why businesses initially got involved in financing and managing employee health insurance. U.S. businesses first got involved in health insurance because of government price controls. The federal government froze industrial wages during World War II, forbidding companies to increase wages. The price controls, however, did not apply to fringe benefits. Businesses found that the only way to legally compensate workers at increased rates was to increase fringe benefits, one of which was health insurance. Businesses continue to finance many workers' health insurance benefits. In 1994 nearly 53 percent of all employees were enrolled in an employer-sponsored or union-backed group health plan.

There are some financial advantages for insurers and workers in purchasing health insurance through employer-sponsored group plans. Washington Consumers' Checkbook, a nonprofit organization that evaluates health plans, summarized those advantages:

> Some health plans offer coverage at lower rates to employed groups than to individuals. The plans offer these better rates because they believe employed persons are less likely to be sick than are persons who aren't working. Also, they know that by insuring a group they can expect to get some healthy individuals, not just unhealthy individuals who particularly want insurance. In addition, they allow for the fact that dealing with a group rather than individuals reduces administrative costs.

Today, however, the ever-increasing costs of health care are leading businesses to reconsider their role in financing health insurance. The number of businesses that finance the total cost of health insurance has declined over the last decade. In 1980, 74 percent of employers who provided health insurance financed the entire package—that is, they did not require any employee contributions. By 1993 that number dropped to 37 percent.

HOW THE TAX CODE DISTORTS THE HEALTH CARE MARKET

While there is no doubt that Americans have lost control over their selection of health care benefits during the past decade, some economists argue that Americans have voluntarily given up their health freedom. They claim that if employees do not like the choice of providers and treatments covered under their employer-sponsored health insurance plan, they are free to buy another plan. For example, it has been noted that federal employees voluntarily purchase their health insurance through the Federal Employee Health Benefits Program (FEHBP). No law requires federal employees or other workers to purchase health insurance through their employers. But the current tax law does force workers to pay higher taxes if they buy health insurance on their own. A worker earning $25,000 per year would have to pay $540 more for health insurance if he purchased it individually rather than through his employer. In that way, the government manipulates the health insurance market, making employer-based insurance the preferred option for workers.

The major problem with today's health insurance tax law is summarized by Rashi Fein, professor of the economics of medicine at Harvard Medical School:

> The influence of the way the tax system allocates its rewards and exacts its penalties should never be underestimated. Just as home ownership is stimulated by the deductibility of mortgage interest and local property tax payments, so the development of health insurance was stimulated by the tax code. But in addition, the code provided an incentive that shaped a particular (and inequitable) set of institutional arrangements. It did not assist individual enrollment or even group enrollment per se (such as neighborhood, religious, or fraternal associations). Rather, it subsidized the purchase of health insurance only when the employer paid the premium. It thus linked health insurance to employment. In doing so, the tax code molded the nature of American health insurance, its availability and distribution. In extending benefits to some, the tax code discriminated against others.

HIGHER COSTS, FEWER CHOICES

Nobel laureate economist Milton Friedman explains that the current tax law affects the cost and choice of health care benefits in two ways: (1) It leads workers to rely on employers, rather than themselves, to finance and manage health care. (2) It leads workers to take a larger fraction of total compensation in the form of health care. Friedman concludes,

> If the tax exemption [for health insurance] were removed, employees could bargain with their employers for higher take-home pay in lieu of health care, and provide for their own health care, either by dealing directly with health care providers or through purchasing health insurance.

The current tax law also encourages workers to join HMOs. In cases in which employers offer insurance only through an HMO, workers are forced to choose the HMO or forgo the tax exclusion for health insurance altogether. Thus, most people accept the health insurance plans offered by their employers, even if that means joining an HMO. Scott Holleran, executive director of Americans for Free Choice in Medicine, notes,

> Government virtually created managed care in the form of HMOs and encourages them through a tax code that forces Americans to get their health insurance through their employer. Don't blame the market for what the government has done to our system. The free market didn't create HMOs; government did.

The growth in HMOs did not occur in the free market; it was spawned by federal legislation in 1973. Backed by the Nixon administration and Sen. Edward Kennedy (D-Mass.), the HMO legislation required employers to offer workers the option of joining an HMO. The number of Americans enrolled in HMOs grew from 6 million in 1976 to more than 46 million in 1995. Today, some 70 percent of private employees are enrolled in some form of managed care. Keep in mind that employers often determine the price a worker pays for health insurance, so employers can set prices that encourage workers to join HMOs. The true demand for HMOs remains unknown, given that the federal tax law and HMO legislation have distorted the market. . . .

A Universal Tax Credit for Health Insurance

The best way to reform the tax treatment of health insurance would be to implement a flat-rate income tax or a national sales tax. Either of those tax policies would render neutral the federal government's tax treatment of all goods and services, including health care. However, in the absence of fundamental tax reform, the most politically viable policy solution would be to implement a universal tax credit for health insurance.

Instead of continuing the current employer-based tax exclusion policy that limits employees' choice of health plans, the government should eliminate it and replace it with a universal tax credit. Unlike current tax exemptions, a universal tax credit would neither discriminate against those who purchased health insurance individually (by giving a preference to those who purchased insurance through employers) nor reward those who paid for health care services through insurance rather than out of pocket. A universal tax credit would render neutral the government's treatment of health insurance taxation, thus allowing individuals to purchase health insurance and health care in the way that best meets their needs. . . .

The universal tax credit for health insurance is an efficient and fair way to help Americans gain greater control over their health care choices. If individuals did not like the choice of providers and treatments covered under their employer-sponsored health insurance plans, they would be free to buy other plans without paying higher taxes. That is especially important for the 48 percent of American workers who are offered only one health plan. The universal tax credit should be considered a viable policy option for covering the uninsured while restoring health freedom for all individuals.

PERIODICAL BIBLIOGRAPHY

The following articles have been selected to supplement the diverse views presented in this chapter. Addresses are provided for periodicals not indexed in the *Readers' Guide to Periodical Literature*, the *Alternative Press Index*, the *Social Sciences Index*, or the *Index to Legal Periodicals and Books*.

Henry J. Aaron	"End of an Era: The New Debate over Health Care Financing," *Brookings Review*, Winter 1996.
Pat and Hugh Armstrong with Claudia Fegan	"The Best Solution: Questions and Answers on Canada's Health Care System," *Washington Monthly*, June 1998.
Stuart M. Butler	"Patient Approach," *National Review*, March 6, 1995.
Stuart M. Butler and Robert E. Moffit	"Congress's Own Health Plan as a Model for Medicare Reform," *Heritage Foundation Backgrounder*, June 12, 1997. Available from 214 Massachussets Ave. NE, Washington, DC 20002-4999 or http://www.heritage.org.
Craig J. Cantoni	"The Case Against Employee Benefits," *Wall Street Journal*, August 18, 1997.
Theodore Dalrymple	"The Price Britain Pays for Free Health Care," *Wall Street Journal*, July 21, 1998.
Robert Dreyfuss and Peter H. Stone	"Medikill," *Mother Jones*, January/February 1996.
Michael S. Dukakis	"Health Care Reform: Not a Dead Issue," *America*, May 10, 1997.
James K. Glassman	"A Nonsurgical Fix for Health Care," *U.S. News & World Report*, May 5, 1997.
David B. Kendall and Mark V. Pauly	"Health Care Reform Starts with Tax Reform," *Wall Street Journal*, June 6, 1996.
Bart Laws	"Health vs. Medicine: Where Do We Go from Here with Health Care Reform?" *Z Magazine*, July/August 1998.
Steven A. Lyons	"Bob Dole in the Year 2025," *Z Magazine*, February 1996.
Joseph Weber	"Canada's Health-Care System Isn't a Model Anymore," *Business Week*, August 24–31, 1998.

GLOSSARY

adverse selection The tendency of persons who present a poorer-than-average health risk to apply for, or continue, insurance to a greater extent than do persons with average or better-than-average expectations of health.

benefit package The covered services each patient is entitled to under a **managed care** contract.

capitation An arrangement in which **managed care** plans pay a fixed monthly or annual fee to physicians for each patient in their care. Doctors receive the same fixed amount each month regardless of how much care the plan member receives.

claim A request by either an individual or his or her physician asking an insurance company to pay for services the insured obtained from a health care professional.

copayment the percentage or proportion of a health insurance claim that is paid directly "out of pocket" by the patient.

deductible the fixed amount of money that an individual must pay before the insurance company will begin to reimburse for services.

fee-for-service The traditional way of paying for medical services. Doctors in private practice charge a fee for each service provided, and the patient's insurer pays all or part of that fee.

gatekeeper A health care professional (usually a physician) responsible for coordinating a patient's utilization of services and controlling access to specialists and procedures. The primary purpose of having a gatekeeper is to control costs and prevent unnecessary utilization of services.

health maintenance organization (HMO) A **managed care** plan that provides health care in return for preset monthly payments. Physicians in these plans share in the financial risk for the delivery of health services, and enrollees typically are not covered to see physicians who do not have a contract with the HMO.

managed care A variety of health care financing and delivery systems that are designed to limit costs and control use of health care services. Some managed care plans attempt to improve health quality by emphasizing prevention of disease.

Medicaid A combined federal- and state-funded program that provides health care for the indigent population (individuals living below the poverty line). Medicaid was established in 1965 under the Social Security Act to help reduce the number of uninsured Americans.

Medicare A federal entitlement program that provides health care benefits to individuals who are over sixty-five years of age, blind, disabled, or have renal disease. Medicare Part A provides coverage for hospital visits and Medicare Part B provides physician visits, pharmacy, and other health services. Medicare is an entitlement program—everybody who falls into one of the previously mentioned categories automatically receives benefits. However, individuals who receive Medicare must pay **deductibles**, **premiums**, and **copayments** to receive services. Medicare was established in 1965 as part of the Social Security Act.

outpatient A patient who receives health care services (such as surgery) on an outpatient basis, meaning they do not stay overnight in a hospital or inpatient facility. Many insurance companies have identified a list of tests and procedures (including surgery) that will not be covered (paid for) unless they are performed on an outpatient basis.

point-of-service option A provision in some **HMO** contracts that allows patients to choose to pay extra in order to have the **HMO** provide coverage for services rendered by physicians who are not included in the health plan's network.

pre-existing condition A medical condition that is excluded from coverage by an insurance company because the condition was believed to exist prior to the individual obtaining a policy from the particular insurance company.

premium   The (usually monthly) sum paid by a policyholder to keep his or her insurance policy in force.

primary care physician   *See* **gatekeeper**

provider   Any health professional who provides medical-related services. This broader term is often used in place of *doctor* or *physician* to encompass registered nurses, therapists, hospitals, dentists, etc.

third-party payment   Payment of medical services by an entity other than the individual receiving the services or the provider of the services. An example of third-party payment is reimbursement by an insurance company or the federal government through the **Medicare** program to a doctor or hospital. The third party is not directly involved with the delivery of service.

FOR FURTHER DISCUSSION

CHAPTER 1

1. Joseph A. Califano Jr. maintains that the United States has "the finest system for treating illnesses and injuries in the world." Does Steven Kangas actually disagree with this statement? Or do the two authors interpret "health care system" to mean different things?

2. Advances in medicine have saved the lives of millions of people, yet Willard Gaylin blames these very advances for rising health care costs. Do you believe, as he does, that expensive medical procedures should be rationed? Defend your answer.

3. Consider the American Medical Student Association's argument that health care should be a right, together with Robert Pear's description of the problem of the uninsured. Do you believe Americans should have a right to health care? Now consider Willard Gaylin's argument that health care must be rationed, together with Sheldon Richman's view that the government should not be put in charge of rationing health care. Based on these viewpoints, do you think the plight of the uninsured outweighs the possible dangers of government-controlled health care?

CHAPTER 2

1. According to Susan Brink, what trends in the U.S. health care system led to the widespread growth of managed health care that began in the 1980s? How does Ronald J. Glasser explain the rise of managed care? In your opinion, whose explanation is more plausible? Are the two histories compatible? Explain your answers.

2. In his viewpoint, David Jacobsen discusses the innovations and policies that his own HMO has adopted, then cites statistics indicating that most people are satisfied with their health care. Which part of his viewpoint do you find more persuasive? Deborah A. Stone makes a more abstract argument, contending that the fundamental principles of managed care harm the doctor-patient relationship. Whose argument is more convincing, and why?

CHAPTER 3

1. Brian J. LeClair believes that if health plans are required to guarantee certain benefits, they will raise their premiums and more people will be unable to afford health insurance. For the sake of argument, assume that each of the patient protections described

by Barbara Boxer would increase premiums enough that health insurance becomes unaffordable for 60,000 Americans (roughly 0.1 percent of those currently enrolled in managed care plans). In your opinion, which of the patient protection provisions are worth this cost, and which are not? Do you believe that some of the provisions should be adopted regardless of cost?

2. Karen Ignagni is president of a trade group that represents managed care organizations. Does her occupation make her views seem more or less credible than those of Linda Peeno, who left her position at a managed care organization because she believes it pressured her into making unethical medical decisions? Why or why not?

3. James Moore believes that governments should set health goals for their populations and establish a plan to meet them. In addition to the "fat tax" and other measures described by Jacob Sullum, how might the government try to meet the health goals Moore describes? Do you agree with Sullum that such measures would constitute unjust government intrusion into people's personal decisions? Or do you believe, as Moore does, that the government ought to promote the health of its citizens? Address the issue of rising health care costs in your answer.

CHAPTER 4

1. The type of health care reform a person prefers depends on what that individual believes the goal of health care reform should be. One goal has been to reduce the cost of health care—this has been the impetus behind the shift to managed care. Another goal is to increase people's choices in health care. Still another goal of reform is to help the 41 million Americans who do not have health insurance. Which of these goals do you feel is most important? Which of the reforms described in this chapter do you think best achieves each of these three goals, and which of the reforms do you think would most benefit the health care system?

2. Advocates of employer-provided insurance note that when insurance is purchased by a group, the entire group is charged the same premium. When individuals purchase insurance, the insurer may vary their premiums based on the risk that each person represents, and may deny insurance to people with higher health risks, such as the elderly and people with pre-existing conditions. In his criticism of medical savings accounts, Jonathan Cohn contends that "deep down, for-profit insurance companies don't really want to take care of sick people." Based on his viewpoint, what might Cohn feel were

the advantages and disadvantages of Sue Blevins's plan to make individually owned health insurance more affordable?

3. Many advocates of national health insurance believe that the program must be mandatory—or at least that everyone must pay taxes to support it—so that the risks can be spread across the largest possible number of people. This compulsory aspect is also what many people find most objectionable about national health insurance: Michael Hurd quotes one critic of Canada's system as saying, "The public doesn't want a high quality medical system, it wants a free system." In your opinion, do the benefits of national health insurance, as described by Pat and Hugh Armstrong and David DeGrazia, outweigh the injustice that many people would feel in being forced to participate in the program?

GENERAL QUESTION

1. In Chapter 1, the American Medical Student Association argues that governments should provide their citizens with health care; Sheldon Richman warns that the government should not be allowed to ration health care. In Chapter 2, Stephen Chapman and Michael W. Lynch argue that free-market competition will improve the managed care system, while in Chapter 3, Barbara Boxer contends that government regulation of HMOs is necessary. Finally, in Chapter 4, Pat and Hugh Armstrong argue that Canada's government does a fairer, more efficient job of rationing health care than America's private insurers do, whereas Michael J. Hurd claims that government control of health care in Canada has been disastrous. Can you find other viewpoints in this book in which the author reveals a strong faith in either government or free-market capitalism? How does it affect their viewpoints?

ORGANIZATIONS TO CONTACT

The editors have compiled the following list of organizations concerned with the issues debated in this book. The descriptions are derived from materials provided by the organizations. All have publications or information available for interested readers. The list was compiled on the date of publication of the present volume; the information provided here may change. Be aware that many organizations take several weeks or longer to respond to inquiries, so allow as much time as possible.

Ad Hoc Committee to Defend Health Care
649 Massachusetts Ave., Suite 8, Cambridge, MA 02139
(617) 576-7741 • fax: (617) 354-1961
website: http://www.defendhealthcare.org

The committee is a group of doctors and nurses that encourages a broad public dialogue about the structuring and financing of health care services and works toward reform in the current health care system. The Ad Hoc Committee to Defend Health Care offers numerous newspaper and journal articles, including "The Call to Action," its position statement on the effects of managed care.

American Public Health Association (APHA)
1015 15th St. NW, Washington, DC 20005-2605
(202) 789-5600 • fax: (202) 789-5661
e-mail: comments@apha.org • website: http://www.apha.org

Founded in 1872, the American Public Health Association consists of over fifty-thousand individuals and organizations that support health promotion. Its members represent over fifty public health occupations, including researchers, practitioners, administrators, teachers, and other health care workers. Some of APHA's publications include Control of Communicable Diseases Manual, Standard Methods for the Examination of Water and Wastewater, and Chronic Disease Epidemiology and Control.

American Society of Law, Medicine & Ethics (ASLME)
765 Commonwealth Ave., Suite 1634, Boston, MA 02215
(617) 262-4990 • fax: (617) 437-7596
e-mail: info@aslme.org • website: http://www.aslme.org

The mission of ASLME is to provide high-quality scholarship, debate, and critical thought to professionals in the fields of law, health care, policy, and ethics. The society acts as a source of guidance and information through the publication of two quarterlies, the Journal of Law, Medicine & Ethics and the American Journal of Law & Medicine. More information about ALSME is available at its website.

Brookings Institution
1775 Massachusetts Ave. NW, Washington, DC 20036
(202) 797-6000 • fax: (202) 797-6004
website: http://www.brook.edu

Founded in 1927, the institution is a liberal research and education organization that publishes material on economics, government, and foreign policy. It strives to serve as a bridge between scholarship and public policy, bringing new knowledge to the attention of decision makers and providing scholars with improved insight into public policy issues. The Brookings Institution produces hundreds of abstracts and reports on health care with topics ranging from Medicaid to persons with disabilities.

Cato Institute

1000 Massachusetts Ave. NW, Washington, DC 20001-5403
(202) 842-0200 • fax: (202) 842-3490
e-mail: cato@cato.org • website: http://www.cato.org

The institute is a libertarian public policy research foundation dedicated to limiting the role of government and protecting individual liberties. Their Health and Welfare Studies department works to formulate and popularize a free-market agenda for health care reform. The institute publishes the quarterly magazine *Regulation*, the bimonthly *Cato Policy Report*, and numerous books and commentaries, hundreds of which relate to health care.

Healthcare Leadership Council (HLC)

900 17th St. NW, Suite 600, Washington, DC 20006
(202) 452-8700
website: http://www.hlc.org

The council is a forum in which health care industry leaders can jointly develop policies, plans, and programs that support a market-based health care system. HLC believes America's health care system should value innovation and provide affordable high-quality health care free from excessive government regulations. It offers the latest press releases on health issues and several public policy papers with titles such as "Empowering Consumers and Patients" and "Ensuring Responsible Government."

Heritage Foundation

214 Massachusetts Ave. NE, Washington, DC 20002-4999
(800) 544-4843 • (202) 546-4400 • fax: (202) 544-6979
e-mail: pubs@heritage.org • website: http://www.heritage.org

The foundation is a public policy research institute that advocates limited government and the free market system. It believes the private sector, not government, should be relied upon to ease social problems. The Heritage Foundation publishes the quarterly *Policy Review* as well as hundreds of monographs, books, and background papers with titles such as "Medicare Minus Choice" and "What to Do About Uninsured Children."

Institute for Health Freedom (IHF)

1155 Connecticut Ave. NW, Suite 300, Washington, DC 20036
(202) 429-6610 • fax: (202) 861-1973
website: http://www.forhealthfreedom.org

The institute is a nonpartisan, nonprofit research center established to bring the issues of personal freedom in choosing health care to the forefront of America's health policy debate. Its mission is to present the ethical and economic case for strengthening personal health freedom. IHF's research and analyses are published as policy briefings on subjects such as "Children's Health Care," "Monopoly in Medicine," and "Legal Issues." All are available through its website.

National Center for Policy Analysis (NCPA)
655 15th St. NW, Suite 375, Washington, DC 20005
(202) 628-6671 • fax: (202) 628-6474
e-mail: ncpa@public-policy.org • website: http://www.ncpa.org
NCPA is a nonprofit public policy research institute. It publishes the bimonthly newsletter *Executive Alert* as well as numerous health care policy studies with titles such as "Saving Medicare" and "Medical Savings Accounts: Obstacles to Their Growth and Ways to Improve Them," and its website includes an extensive section on health care issues.

National Coalition on Health Care
555 13th St. NW, Washington, DC 20004
(202) 637-6830 • fax: (202) 637-6861
website: http://www.nchc.org

The National Coalition on Health Care is a nonprofit, nonpartisan group that represents the nation's largest alliance working to improve America's health care and make it more affordable. The coalition offers several policy studies with titles ranging from "Why the Quality of U.S. Health Care Must Be Improved" to "The Rising Number of Uninsured Workers: An Approaching Crisis in Health Care Financing."

Nurses' Network for a National Health Program
3325 S. Michigan Ave., Suite 500, Chicago, IL 60604-4302
(312) 554-0382 • fax: (312) 554-0383
website: http://ideanurse.com/nnnhp

The network is a national group of nurses dedicated to creating a universal health care system that serves the needs of all patients. It endorses a single-payer, not-for-profit national health insurance model and offers a book entitled *The National Health Program Reader*, which documents articles about single-payer health care.

Urban Institute
2100 M St. NW, Washington, DC 20037
(202) 261-5244
website: http://www.urban.org

The Urban Institute investigates social and economic problems confronting the nation and analyzes efforts to solve these problems. In addition, the institute works to improve government decisions and their implementations and to increase citizen awareness about important public choices. It offers a wide variety of resources, including books such as *Restructuring Medicare: Impacts on Beneficiaries* and *The Decline in Medical Spending Growth in 1996: Why Did It Happen?*

BIBLIOGRAPHY OF BOOKS

Henry J. Aaron, ed. — *The Problem That Won't Go Away: Reforming U.S. Health Care Financing.* Washington, DC: Brookings Institution, 1996.

Stuart H. Altman, Uwe E. Reinhardt, and Alexandra E. Shields, eds. — *The Future U.S. Healthcare System: Who Will Care for the Poor and the Uninsured?* Chicago: Health Administration Press, 1998.

George Anders — *Health Against Wealth: HMOs and the Breakdown of Medical Trust.* New York: Houghton Mifflin, 1996.

Charles Andrews — *Profit Fever: The Drive to Corporatize Health Care and How to Stop It.* Monroe, ME: Common Courage Press, 1995.

Pat and Hugh Armstrong with Claudia Fegan — *Universal Health Care: What the United States Can Learn from the Canadian Experience.* New York: New Press, 1998.

Ellen Davidson Baer, Claire M. Fagin, and Suzanne Gordon, eds. — *Abandonment of the Patient: The Impact of Profit-Driven Health Care on the Public.* New York: Springer, 1996.

Dan E. Beauchamp — *Health Care Reform and the Battle for the Body Politic.* Philadelphia: Temple University Press, 1996.

Beverly Lieff Benderly — *In Her Own Right: The Institute of Medicine's Guide to Women's Health Issues.* Washington, DC: National Academy Press, 1997.

Arnold Birenbaum — *Managed Care: Made in America.* Westport, CT: Praeger, 1997.

Daniel Callahan — *False Hopes: Why America's Quest for Perfect Health Is a Recipe for Failure.* New York: Simon & Schuster, 1998.

John Canham-Clyne et al. — *The Rational Option for a National Health Program.* Westport, CT: Pamphleteers Press, 1995.

John J. Connolly — *The ABCs of HMOs: How to Get the Best from Managed Care.* Allentown, PA: Peoples Medical Society, 1997.

Norman Daniels — *Seeking Fair Treatment: From the AIDS Epidemic to National Health Care Reform.* New York: Oxford University Press, 1995.

Peter Davis, ed. — *Contested Ground: Public Purpose and Private Interest in the Regulation of Prescription Drugs.* New York: Oxford University Press, 1996.

Charles J. Dougherty — *Back to Reform: Values, Markets, and the Health Care System.* New York: Oxford University Press, 1996.

Richard Epstein | *Mortal Peril: Our Inalienable Right to Health Care?* Reading, MA: Addison-Wesley, 1997.

Miguel A. Faria Jr. | *Medical Warrior: Fighting Corporate Socialized Medicine.* Macon, GA: Hacienda, 1997.

Miguel A. Faria Jr. | *Vandals at the Gates of Medicine: Historic Perspectives on the Battle over Health Care Reform.* Macon, GA: Hacienda, 1995.

Stephen M. Fried | *Bitter Pills: Inside the Hazardous World of Legal Drugs.* New York: Bantam Doubleday Dell, 1998.

Michael Fumento | *The Fat of the Land: Our Health Crisis and How Overweight Americans Can Help Themselves.* New York: Penguin USA, 1998.

Sherry Glied | *Chronic Condition: Why Health Reform Fails.* Cambridge, MA: Harvard University Press, 1997.

Martin L. Gross | *The Medical Racket: How Doctors, HMOs, and Hospitals Are Failing the American Patient.* New York: Avon Books, 1998.

Jacob S. Hacker | *The Road to Nowhere: The Genesis of President Clinton's Plan for Health Security.* Princeton, NJ: Princeton University Press, 1997.

Chris Hackler, ed. | *Health Care for an Aging Population.* New York: State University of New York Press, 1994.

Max Heirich | *Rethinking Health Care: Innovation and Change in America.* Boulder, CO: Westview Press, 1998.

Regina E. Herzlinger | *Market-Driven Health Care: Who Wins, Who Loses in the Transformation of America's Largest Service Industry.* Reading, MA: Perseus, 1997.

David J. Hunter | *Desperately Seeking Solutions: Rationing Health Care.* New York: Addison-Wesley, 1998.

Haynes Johnson and David S. Broder | *The System: The American Way of Politics at the Breaking Point.* Boston: Little, Brown, 1997.

John F. Kilner, Robert D. Orr, and Judy Allen Shelly, eds. | *The Changing Face of Health Care: A Christian Appraisal of Managed Care, Resource Allocation, and Patient-Caregiver Relationships.* Grand Rapids, MI: William B. Eerdmans, 1998.

J.D. Kleinke | *Bleeding Edge: The Business of Health Care in the New Century.* Gaithersburg, MD: Aspen, 1998.

Nicholas Laham | *A Lost Cause: Bill Clinton's Campaign for National Health Insurance.* Westport, CT: Praeger, 1996.

John Langone | *Harvard Med: The Story Behind America's Premier Medical School and the Making of America's Doctors.* New York: Crown, 1995.

John D. Lantos	*Do We Still Need Doctors?* New York: Routledge, 1997.
Bernard Lown	*The Lost Art of Healing.* Boston: Houghton Mifflin, 1996.
Antonia Maioni	*Parting at the Crossroads: The Emergence of Health Insurance in the United States and Canada.* Princeton, NJ: Princeton University Press, 1998.
Lynne McTaggart	*What Doctors Don't Tell You: The Truth About the Dangers of Modern Medicine.* New York: Avon Books, 1998.
Kary L. Moss, ed.	*Man-Made Medicine: Women's Health, Public Policy, and Reform.* Durham, NC: Duke University Press, 1996.
Susan Murphy	*I Hate Doctors: 225 Reasons Why You Should, Too.* Birmingham, AL: Crane Hill, 1997.
Lynn Payer	*Disease-Mongers: How Doctors, Drug Companies, and Insurers Are Making You Feel Sick.* New York: John Wiley & Sons, 1994.
Curtis Prout	*Demand and Get the Best Health Care for You: An Eminent Doctor's Practical Advice.* Winchester, MA: Faber & Faber, 1996.
Marilynn M. Rosenthal, ed.	*Health Policy: Understanding Our Choices from National Reform to Market Force.* Boulder, CO: Westview Press, 1998.
David Seedhouse, ed.	*Reforming Health Care: The Philosophy and Practice of International Health Reform.* New York: John Wiley & Sons, 1995.
Theda Skocpol	*Boomerang: Clinton's Health Security Effort and the Turn Against Government in U.S. Politics.* New York: W.W. Norton, 1996.
Jacob Sullum	*For Your Own Good: The Anti-Smoking Crusade and the Tyranny of Public Health.* New York: Free Press, 1998.
Warner V. Slack	*Cybermedicine: How Computing Empowers Doctors and Patients for Better Health Care.* New York: Jossey-Bass, 1997.
Neil Vidmar	*Medical Malpractice and the American Jury: Confronting the Myths About Jury Incompetence, Deep Pockets, and Outrageous Damage Awards.* Ann Arbor: University of Michigan Press, 1996.
Joseph White	*Competing Solutions: American Health Care Proposals and International Experience.* Washington, DC: Brookings Institution, 1995.
John R. Wolfe	*The Coming Health Crisis: Who Will Pay for Care for the Aged in the Twenty-First Century?* Chicago: University of Chicago Press, 1993.

INDEX